Super Soya

Recipes and facts for greater health

Super Soya

Tanya Carr and Joanna Farrow

hamlyn

First published in Great Britain in 2005 by Hamlyn,
a division of Octopus Publishing Group Ltd,
2-4 Heron Quays, London, E14 4JP

ISBN 0 600 61192 2
EAN 9780600611929

A CIP catalogue record for this book is available from
the British Library.

Printed and bound in China.

10 9 8 7 6 5 4 3 2 1

Joanna Farrow trained as a home economist and has worked as a
freelance writer for several food magazines. She has also written a
diverse range of cookery books, including *30 Minute Vegetarian* and
Simply Cadbury's Chocolate. She also styles food for book, magazine
and advertising photography.

Tanya Carr (*BSc RD R.Nutr*) is a registered dietitian and nutritionist.
She writes regularly for the medical and health press, appears
frequently on TV and radio and has a private clinic in North London.
She has worked in a variety of posts in the UK National Health Service
as well as in the food and pharmaceutical industry. Tanya runs her
own practice providing nutrition consultancy to the food industry,
healthcare professionals, the media, publishers, charities and other
health organizations.

contents

Introducing Soya

'Soya has been grown and eaten in China for more than 5000 years.'

Over the last few years a huge variety of soya products has begun to appear on the supermarket shelves. Once found only in health-food shops, soya products are now widely available and consumed by increasing numbers of people. As well as whole beans, soya is also sold in a wide range of forms, ranging from tofu and milk to meat alternatives, burgers and snacks, making it a versatile ingredient that can be used in almost any style of cooking. The meal planners and recipes (see pages 22–24 and 28–125) offer quick and easy ways to include soya in your daily diet. This need not involve making major changes in your eating patterns or spending hours in the kitchen – many fantastic soya-based recipes can be made in minutes.

POSSIBLE BENEFITS OF SOYA

- Reduced blood cholesterol levels
- Better heart health
- Maintained healthy weight
- Reduction in severe hot flushes
- Improved energy levels
- Boosted nutrient profile of your diet

WHO CAN BENEFIT FROM EATING SOYA?

Whether you are a vegetarian or a meat-eater, soya is not just a valuable source of protein, but has numerous health benefits, some of which are only just being discovered and understood (see box, left and pages 14–18).

WHAT IS SOYA?

The soya bean, *Glycine Max*, is a member of the legume family, which includes peas, beans and lentils. The plants grow to a height of 80–100 cm (32–40 in) and have clusters of pods in which the beans develop. There are many varieties that are used for different

Soya is becoming more widely cultivated in the west as its health benefits are more generally known.

purposes, including animal feed and green fuel, but the most commonly used for food is the yellow soya bean.

Although soya was only introduced to the west relatively recently, it has been grown in China for more than 5000 years. One ancient Chinese Emperor called soya '*Ta Teou*', which means 'The Big Bean' and today it is often referred to as 'the meat of the soil' in China. Soya first appeared in Europe in the eighteenth century, but it was only in the last part of the twentieth century that some of the real beneficial properties of soya for human health were discovered.

Today, the United States produces some 49 per cent of the world's soya. Brazil produces about 20 per cent and China produces roughly 10 per cent. Other countries that grow significant amounts of soya are Canada, Taiwan, Argentina and India.

Transforming the Bean

'Tofu is an excellent source of protein, fibre, isoflavones and polyunsaturated and essential fats.'

A number of processes are used to transform soya beans into foods or drinks. The beans are processed to produce ingredients that can be used in cooking. The different methods of processing result in differing levels of nutrients.

Whole Soya Beans

These are obviously subject to the least processing. All the goodness remains in the end product. They are available dried and must be soaked before cooking (see page 19).

Soya Flour

There are two varieties: full fat and low fat. Full-fat flour is produced by heating and drying the beans, then grinding them to a fine powder, allowing the majority of nutrients to remain intact. In the low-fat version the beans' oils are extracted before they are ground.

Soya Protein Concentrate

Soya protein concentrates are powders that can be added to foods to increase their protein content. The manufacturing process leaves behind only the protein (about 70 per cent) and the carbohydrate, which gives it flavour.

Soya Protein Isolates

These powders are used to increase protein levels in foods in the same way as soya protein concentrates, but the carbohydrates are also removed during the manufacturing process, leaving a residue of about 90 per cent protein.

Soya flour is one of the many products that can be made by processing the beans.

A SELECTION OF SOYA PRODUCTS AVAILABLE

SOYA MILK ALTERNATIVES

Soya milk is made from soya protein isolate, concentrate or whole soya beans, and is an excellent source of protein and fibre. Soya milk is rich in polyunsaturated and essential fats. It is available both from the chiller cabinet and as long-life versions. The many varieties include those enriched with calcium and vitamins, as well as both sweetened and organic versions. If possible, choose a variety with added calcium.

FLAVOURED SOYA DRINKS

Soya milk is used as the base for these drinks, which are a great alternative to dairy milkshakes.

SOY/SOYA/SHOYU SAUCE

Varieties of soy sauce are made from defatted soya flour, corn syrup and caramel colouring. They are mainly used as a flavouring and contain no protein or isoflavones (see page 11). Light soy sauce tends to contain more salt.

TEMPEH

This is fermented whole soya bean paste, which is used as a meat substitute.

SOYA MINCE

TVP® (Textured Vegetable Protein) is the best-known form of soya mince and meat substitute. It is made from soya flour. Other varieties are available.

MISO

Made from fermented whole soya bean paste and other grains, miso is used as a meat substitute, as well as to flavour soups and stocks.

TOFU

Also known as bean curd, tofu is used as a meat and cheese replacement. It is produced from whole soya beans: varieties include plain, smoked and silken. Tofu is an excellent source of protein, fibre, isoflavones (see page 11) and polyunsaturated and essential fats.

Getting to Know the Bean

'It has long been suspected that the greater life expectancy of people in Japan... has resulted from their diet.'

So why is eating soya beans and soya products so good for our health? Soya beans and many soya foods, including tofu, soya milk and soya nuts, have a unique balance of nutrients that help to promote health and vitality (see box below). It has long been suspected that the greater life expectancy of people in Japan in comparison to the west (especially the low rates of heart disease) has resulted from their diet, in which a large proportion of protein is obtained from soya instead of meat and dairy products.

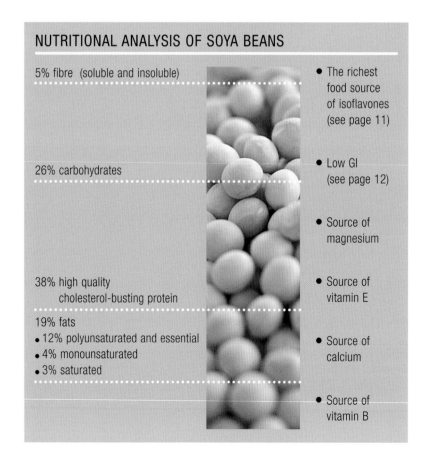

NUTRITIONAL ANALYSIS OF SOYA BEANS

5% fibre (soluble and insoluble)

26% carbohydrates

38% high quality cholesterol-busting protein

19% fats
- 12% polyunsaturated and essential
- 4% monounsaturated
- 3% saturated

- The richest food source of isoflavones (see page 11)
- Low GI (see page 12)
- Source of magnesium
- Source of vitamin E
- Source of calcium
- Source of vitamin B

GREAT THINGS COME IN SMALL PACKAGES

Soya beans may look just like any other small beans, but analysis of their contents reveals that they are lower in carbohydrates and richer in both proteins and isoflavones (see opposite). It is really no coincidence that an increased public awareness of, and consumption of, soya is occurring at the same time as more and more scientific research backs up what people in many Asian countries have long believed – that soya is good for you.

PACKING A PROTEIN PUNCH

It is not simply the quantity of protein in soya that makes it unique:

● It is better than other plant proteins because it is the only one that contains all of the essential amino acids in the correct quantity and quality needed by the body and in this is equal to animal proteins.

● It has been scientifically proven that soya protein is superior to animal protein because it uniquely lowers blood cholesterol (see pages 14–15).

Soya nuts make a high-protein, high-fibre snack that has much less fat than other nuts or crisps.

THE LOWDOWN ON ISOFLAVONES

A lot has been written about isoflavones, but what exactly are they? They are plant chemicals that belong to a group of substances called phytoestrogens. They are similar to the hormone oestrogen and research indicates that they have health benefits for both women and men (see pages 16–18). Phytoestrogens occur in all plants, but the isoflavones in which soya is particularly rich have generated excitement as scientists think that they are responsible for the lower rates of heart disease, breast and prostate cancer, as well as reduced menopausal symptoms seen among people who eat lots of soya.

FILL UP ON FIBRE

Dietitians recommend plenty of fibre in our diet. There are two types: soluble, which lowers blood cholesterol, and insoluble, which is essential for a healthy gut and may help to lower the risk of certain cancers. Soya is rich in both soluble and insoluble fibre.

Beans and wholegrains share their low GI properties with soya. These foods make you feel full for longer.

GOOD CARBS

Scientists have discovered that the carbohydrates in different foods are digested and absorbed into the bloodstream at different rates. They measure this using the 'Glycaemic Index' (GI). High GI foods (such as cakes, biscuits and white bread) are absorbed quickly, causing a sharp increase in blood sugar levels, followed by a drop that leaves you tired and suffering hunger pangs. Low GI foods (including beans, lentils and most fruit and vegetables) take longer to digest, so blood sugar rises and falls slowly and smoothly, giving you steady energy levels. Low GI foods are useful in a balanced weight-loss plan and may help to reduce the risk of type II diabetes.

GREAT FATS

Not all forms of fat are bad for you; in fact, polyunsaturated fats and essential fatty acids (see below and opposite) are good for health.

Polyunsaturated Fat – The One to Eat

Polyunsaturated fats are mainly found in plants and these fats are good for you. Eating polyunsaturated fats rather than saturated ones (see opposite) has been shown to help lower blood cholesterol levels – countries where high levels of polyunsaturated fats are eaten have lower blood cholesterol levels and fewer instances of heart disease. Soya beans are an excellent source of polyunsaturated fat.

Stocking up on Essential Fats

Essential Fatty Acids (EFAs) help to protect against developing blood clots, are vital for brain function and your immune system, and help boost your mood. Your body synthesizes most of the essential fatty acids for itself, but the essential omega-3 and omega-6 must be obtained from food. Oily fish, such as salmon, tuna and mackerel, are well-known sources of omega-3, but whole soya beans are also a rich source of both omega-3 and omega-6.

TIME TO ATTACK SATURATED FAT

A diet that is high in saturated fat, which is obtained mainly from animal sources, is bad for your heart and your circulation. Too much saturated fat increases blood cholesterol levels (see pages 14–15), leading to deposits building up in the blood, arteries and other tissues which, if blocked, can contribute to heart disease and eventually cause a heart attack. As well as the beneficial effect of soya protein on blood cholesterol levels, whole soya beans, and products made using the whole bean, are low in saturated fat and can therefore have a positive effect on the health of your heart. Many other soya products are also low in saturated fat, but always check the label on individual foods. As a general rule, foods that you eat regularly should contain less than 1.5–2 g of saturated fat per portion. Foods to limit would contain 2.5 g of saturated fat per portion and you should avoid any foods that contain more than 5 g of saturated fat per portion.

'Whole soya beans, and many products made using the whole bean, are low in saturated fat and can therefore have a positive effect on the health of your heart.'

Although soya beans are not fat-free, the fats they contain are mostly polyunsaturated, making them a healthy choice.

Soya and Health

'We need to look seriously at diet and lifestyle and make a conscious effort to change them for the better.'

Soya products – such as the dried beans shown here – are thought to be able to reduce your blood cholesterol levels.

The scientific and medical worlds believe that there are specific areas of health that could benefit from greater consumption of soya beans and soya products.

CHOLESTEROL

Cholesterol is a type of fat that serves several functions, such as helping to create cell walls. The liver produces all that we need, using saturated fat from food and excess body fat. The body requires only a small amount of fat to produce enough cholesterol and eating too much saturated fat can lead to high levels of cholesterol in the blood. It was once thought that all cholesterol was 'bad' but it is now divided into two types, according to whether it is being carried by High Density Lipoprotein or Low Density Lipoprotein.

High Density Lipoprotein (HDL)

This chemical mops up excess cholesterol found in the arteries and blood, then takes it to the liver for removal. HDL cholesterol is referred to as 'good cholesterol', as this form of the lipoprotein helps to keep the arteries clean.

Low Density Lipoprotein (LDL)

If HDL is good then excess LDL cholesterol is definitely 'bad'. This form is picked up from the liver and deposited in the blood, arteries and other tissues. Too much LDL cholesterol results in deposits forming on the blood vessel walls. Eventually this may build up so that the vessel becomes blocked, thus preventing blood flowing freely to the heart and brain. Health problems including heart disease, stroke and deep vein thrombosis (DVT) have all been linked to increased levels of LDL cholesterol.

Measuring Up

Cholesterol is measured in units called millimoles (mmol). The maximum blood cholesterol level should not exceed 5 mmol/l. When it reaches 5.0 mmol/l or above, the risk of heart disease increases dramatically. The amount of LDL cholesterol in the blood should not exceed 3.0 mmol/l and the level of HDL cholesterol should be at least 0.9 mmol/l.

Healthy Hearts

Many western countries are looking at ways to cut the incidence of high blood cholesterol and heart disease drastically. This means that we need to look seriously at diet and lifestyle and make a conscious effort to change them for the better. All too often, this does not happen until after someone has had heart problems or even suffered a heart attack, and we really need to be making the changes before it gets to that stage.

Soya and cholesterol

Eating just 25 g (1 oz) of soya protein every day can help to lower blood cholesterol levels. This amount of soya protein can be obtained by eating between three and four servings of soya food a day, which is surprisingly tasty and easy to achieve (see pages 20–24). Because of this many scientists and nutritionists think that incorporating soya into the diets of many people could form a fundamental part of the approach to help reduce the incidence of heart disease.

Soya oil is a good, healthy alternative to the saturated oils that are often used in cooking.

Silken tofu has a distinctive shape and texture. It can be discreetly incorporated in many dishes to add the benefits of soya.

OSTEOPOROSIS

A lot has been written about the possible benefits of soya isoflavones (see page 11) to bone health. Osteoporosis is the thinning of the bones and it mainly occurs in women of menopausal age, because of the sudden drop in levels of the hormone oestrogen in the body. This results in bone calcium leaching out, which makes the bones more fragile and prone to fractures. Because soya isoflavones mimic oestrogen, albeit thousands of times weaker, some researchers believe that eating soya could help to stop or even reverse the loss of calcium. As yet, this research is in its infancy, however, and no official recommendations have been made at the time of going to press.

BREAST AND PROSTATE CANCER

These are other diseases that are far less prevalent in Asian countries than in the west. Again, this has been partly attributed to high soya food consumption and, in particular, soya isoflavones, although there is no conclusive research at this stage.

OBESITY AND DIABETES

These are interlinked and occurrences of both are increasing worldwide at an alarming rate. Recent research has shown that both protein and fibre play a key role in controlling the appetite. This is obviously of importance in weight management and, as soya beans are high in both, they could also form an important part of the management of blood sugar levels that is so important for people suffering from diabetes.

The Menopause

The symptoms experienced with the onset of the menopause have been attributed to reduced levels of the oestrogen hormone in women. Some symptoms are very noticeable and can be distressing, but may just be short-term, and these can include hot flushes and night sweats. However, other more serious symptoms such as increased blood cholesterol levels, heart disease and osteoporosis, can take longer to develop or may go unnoticed by the sufferer until it is too late.

The isoflavones in soya may help women through some of the symptoms of the menopause.

The most common symptom that women first notice and seek help for is hot flushes. The body temperature increases dramatically in seconds, without warning, resulting in discomfort for the sufferer. The body then starts to perspire, in an attempt to reduce the internal temperature, but this can take anything up to an hour to achieve. The frequency of hot flushes obviously varies greatly between different women, but some sufferers can experience as many as ten of them in a single day.

CHANGING TREATMENT

Current medical treatments available for symptoms of the menopause are two varieties of Hormone Replacement Therapy (HRT); one contains oestrogen only and the other has a combination of oestrogen and progesterone.

However, many women have become worried about the potential side effects of HRT and have started turning to more 'natural'

CALCULATING YOUR ISOFLAVONE INTAKE

	SOYA PROTEIN AVERAGE (g)	ISOFLAVONES ESTIMATED (mg)
250 ml (8 fl oz) glass soya milk alternative*	9.0	20
200 g (7 oz) natural yogurt alternative	9.4	21
200 g (7 oz) fruit yogurt alternative	7.4	16
125 g (4 oz) fruit yogurt alternative	4.8	11
200 g (7 oz) dairy-free custard†	6.0	13
100 g (3½ oz) plain (firm) tofu (raw)†	9.0	26
50 g (2 oz) soya beans (boiled)‡	8.0	27
30 g (1½ oz) soya nuts‡	13.0	38
100 g (3½ oz) textured vegetable protein (ready-to-eat)†	9	27

* based on average protein of three soya milk alternatives
† based on Alpro Dairy Free Alternative Products
‡ based on USDA Database, 1999

HEART DISEASE AND THE MENOPAUSE

The death-rate from heart disease quadruples for women when they reach the menopause. One major factor contributing to this is the dramatic increase in blood cholesterol levels, as a result of the loss in body oestrogen at this time.

remedies, and these often include the use of soya products rich in isoflavones. It is obviously important to discuss the condition and any potential treatment with a doctor before deciding which course to follow, but it is believed that some women who suffer from frequent hot flushes may benefit from including 40–100 g of isoflavones in their diet daily (see the chart above to help calculate this). However, it should be stressed that soya is not an alternative to HRT.

REAPING THE BENEFITS

It is believed that if you are using soya foods to ease the symptoms of the menopause, you should persevere for at least 12 weeks in order to experience the benefits.

Cooking Times and Quantities

Soya beans will take longer to cook than most dried beans, so you might find it more convenient to prepare a large quantity at a time. You can then store the cooked beans in the fridge for a couple of days, using them as and when you need them. If you have only a small quantity left, you can add them to almost any stews, casseroles, pizzas, soups or salads.

COOKING

Before starting, you'll need to soak the beans overnight (or for 12 hours) in plenty of cold water. When ready to cook the beans, drain them, place them in a large pan and cover them with plenty of cold water. Bring them to the boil and boil them for 1 hour, then reduce the heat and simmer them very gently, covered, for about 2 hours, until they are tender. Check the water level regularly, topping it up with boiling water if necessary.

Alternatively, after boiling for 1 hour, transfer the beans to an ovenproof dish, still covered with water, and cook them in a preheated oven, 180°C (350°F, Gas Mark 4), for about 2 hours, until they are tender. This means that you can leave them unattended without the risk of the pan boiling dry.

Quantities

As a guide, cooked beans weigh at least twice as much as dried, so 100 g (3½ oz) of dried beans will weigh at least 200 g (7 oz) when cooked. All the following recipes call for a cooked quantity of beans so, if you're starting from scratch, use half of the amount stated.

It is essential to soak soya beans overnight and cook them thoroughly before eating them.

How to Include Soya in Your Diet

Please note that the nutrient content will vary, depending on the manufacturer. Always check the label for the exact nutrient content of the product per serving suggested.

We should be aiming to include 25 g (1 oz) of soya protein in our diets each day, but just how do you go about this? Use the tables below for some ideas of how to substitute the food that you eat everyday with soya products that will help to benefit your health.

CALCULATING YOUR SOYA PROTEIN INTAKE

INSTEAD OF	TRY	SOYA PROTEIN (g)	TIPS
Dairy milk	Soya milk alternative (Varieties include sweetened, unsweetened, organic, with minerals and vitamins. Choose calcium-enriched varieties.)	8–9.3 per 250 ml (8 fl oz) glass	In the west, the average person consumes 450 ml dairy milk per day. If you use soya milk alternative instead, this will provide you with 14–17 g of soya protein per day. Use soya milk alternative: • poured over cereal • to make milky drinks such as cappuccinos and lattes or smoothies • in cooking
Flavoured milk, dairy drinks and milkshakes	Flavoured soya drinks	9 per 250 ml (8 fl oz) glass	Flavoured soya drinks are exceptionally rich and have an excellent taste. Try the chilled variety or long-life options.
Dairy yogurt	Soya dairy-free yogurt alternatives	4.8 per 125 g (4 oz) pot 7–9 per 200 g (7 oz) serving	Look for them in the chiller cabinets, next to the dairy yogurts.
Dairy custard	Soya dairy-free custard	6 per 200 g (7 oz) serving	Serve it chilled, or heat it gently and serve with a fruit pie.
Meat/chicken burger or sausage	Many varieties of TVP® or tofu-based sausage/burger alternatives	7–12 per 100 g (3½ oz) serving	These products are now extremely sophisticated and flavoured with a variety of herbs and spices.

MAKING UP 25 G (1 OZ) SOYA PROTEIN

Here are some quick-reference ideas on how to easily include the required amount of soya protein in your diet each day.

- 3 x 250 ml (8 fl oz) glasses of soya milk alternative

- 100 g (3½ oz) serving soya beans (cooked weight) *plus*
  1 x 125 ml (4 fl oz) pot fruit soya yogurt alternative *plus*
  1 smoothie made with 250 ml (8 fl oz) soya milk alternative

- 1 x 250 ml (8 fl oz) glass soya milk alternative *plus*
  75 g (3 oz) serving tofu *plus*
  1 x 200 ml (7 fl oz) soya dairy-free custard

- 1 x 250 ml (8 fl oz) glass soya milk alternative *plus*
  1 x 200 ml (7 fl oz) soya yogurt alternative *plus*
  1 x 100 g (3½ oz) rehydrated TVP® serving

- 1 x 250 ml (8 fl oz) glass soya milk alternative *plus*
  1 x 30 g (1½ oz) serving soya nuts *plus*
  1 x 125 ml (4 fl oz) natural soya yogurt alternative

INSTEAD OF	TRY	SOYA PROTEIN (g)	TIPS
Minced meat	TVP® mince	7–12 per 100 g (3½ oz) serving	Try different varieties to find out which you prefer. Most packs come with excellent recipe ideas.
Meat and poultry	Plain (firm) tofu	12 per 100 g (3½ oz) serving	This is now readily available in supermarkets. Chop or thickly slice the tofu, marinate it in soy sauce or ready-made marinade, then stir-fry, bake or grill it.
Cream cheese, sour cream, double cream	Silken tofu	7 per 100 g (3½ oz) serving	Silken tofu has the consistency of thick cream or cream cheese. Use it to make smoothies, on jacket potatoes, in dips or in cheesecakes.
Ready-meals	Chilled, frozen or fresh TVP® or tofu-based products	7–12 per serving	Although ready-meals are not ideal, we all run out of time and they are convenient. A variety of soya-based ready-meals is now available.
Crisps and snacks	Soya nuts	12 per 30 g (1½ oz) serving	Rather than a high calorie snack, try soya nuts. They are available from health-food stores.
Hard cheese and meat	Plain or smoked tofu	7 per 100 g (3½ oz) serving	Marinate plain tofu and pan fry it before use, or choose smoked tofu. Sprinkle over salads, use as a sandwich filling, or on jacket potatoes.

Menu Planners

Here are some daily menu planners, using some of the recipes starting on page 28. Many of the recipes use soya in a form that you won't even notice so you won't feel as if you're eating the same thing for three meals every day. Protein levels are given per average serving and isoflavone levels are an estimate, as they vary from food to food, depending on growing conditions and manufacturing. Please check with individual manufacturers as these menus are only a guide.

MEAL	SOYA PROTEIN (g)	ISOFLAVONES ESTIMATE (mg)
BREAKFAST		
Wholemeal Toast with Scrambled Eggs	00	00
Fruit Juice	00	00
MID-MORNING SNACK		
Piece of fruit	00	00
LUNCH		
Roasted Peppers with Tapenade (page 66)	5.0	11–16
Aromatic Fruit Salad with Ginger (page 81)	2.0	4–7
MID-AFTERNOON SNACK		
30 g (1½ oz) soya nuts	14	31–46
DINNER		
Salmon with Bean and Celeriac Mash (page 112)	9	20–30
Poached Pears	00	00
TOTAL	30	66–99

MEAL	SOYA PROTEIN (g)	ISOFLAVONES ESTIMATE (mg)
BREAKFAST		
Creamy Blueberry Porridge (page 36)	6.0	13–20
MID-MORNING SNACK		
Piece of fruit	00	00
LUNCH		
Salmon sandwich	00	00
125 ml (4 fl oz) of soya yogurt	4.8	11–16
MID-AFTERNOON SNACK		
30 g (1½ oz) soya nuts	14	31–46
DINNER		
Chicken salad with new potatoes	00	00
Banana and Maple Syrup Cake (page 123)	1.3	3–4
TOTAL	26.1	58–86

MEAL	SOYA PROTEIN (g)	ISOFLAVONES ESTIMATE (mg)
BREAKFAST		
Poached egg on toast	00	00
Fruit juice	00	00
MID-MORNING SNACK		
250 ml (8 fl oz) chilled flavoured soya drink	9.5	21–31
LUNCH		
Chicken and salad wholemeal sandwich	00	00
Fruit	00	00
MID-AFTERNOON SNACK		
Handful of dried fruit and nuts	00	00
DINNER		
Tempeh Balti (page 104)	13	29–43
Frozen Toffee Marble Cream (page 118)	4	9–13
TOTAL	26.5	59–87

MEAL	SOYA PROTEIN (g)	ISOFLAVONES ESTIMATE (mg)
BREAKFAST Wholemeal toast and a lean rasher of bacon	00	00
MID-MORNING SNACK Piece of fruit	00	00
LUNCH Citrus Chicken Salad with Beans (page 60)	13	29–43
MID-AFTERNOON SNACK Small handful of olives	00	00
DINNER Fragrant Pilaf (page 88)	13	29–43
Fruit salad	00	00
TOTAL	26	58–86

MEAL	SOYA PROTEIN (g)	ISOFLAVONES ESTIMATE (mg)
BREAKFAST Luxury Fruit and Nut Muesli (page 38)	4.0–7.0	15–23
MID-MORNING SNACK Piece of fruit	00	00
LUNCH Mushroom Soup and Soda Bread	00	00
Lemon Yogurt Ice (page 82)	6.0	13–20
MID-AFTERNOON SNACK 250 ml (8 fl oz) Soya Latte	8.0	18–26
DINNER Shredded Pork and Bean Salad with Sage (see page 97)	11	24–36
Baked Apple	00	00
TOTAL	29–32	79–118

Your Questions Answered

CAN I GIVE MY CHILD REGULAR SOYA MILK ALTERNATIVES?

Newborn to one year

At this age, only breast milk or formula milk should be used as the main source of milk, but once your baby is six months old calcium-enriched soya products can be introduced as part of a healthy, balanced, solid diet. Regular soya milk should not be used as a main milk source at this time.

One to two years

Adult soya milk alternatives should still not be used as the main form of milk for children under the age of two especially because of its low fat content compared to breast milk or milk formula, but soya foods and drinks can be used as part of the child's mixed, balanced diet.

Two years and older

From two years, healthy children who are developing well and follow a balanced diet need less fat, so soya milk alternatives may be used.

CAN I GIVE SOYA INFANT FORMULA TO MY BABY?

You should discuss this with your doctor and registered dietitian. A recent report by the Committee on Toxicity of the Food Standards Agency advised that soya infant formulas should only be used on the advice of a doctor or registered dietitian for medical reasons. Breast milk is the ideal milk for your baby, as it contains essential nutrients, antibodies and healthy bacteria that are so important for the baby's development.

IS SOYA SAFE FOR MY CHILDREN?

There has been some negative publicity regarding soya isoflavones and their safety for children and adults. The concern centres around the use of soya infant formulas and isoflavone capsules. However, all studies demonstrate that the consumption of whole soya foods, such as soya milk alternatives, tofu and textured vegetable proteins is good for you. Always discuss your children's diet with a registered dietitian and their doctor. Isoflavone capsules are not recommended: it is better to obtain their benefits from food.

IF I SWAP MY DAIRY MILK FOR A SOYA MILK ALTERNATIVE, WILL I LACK CALCIUM?

Although the soya bean is a rich source of calcium, soya milk alternatives have very low levels of it unless they have been fortified, as the product is diluted. You should always select a soya milk alternative with added calcium. Most of these will be fortified to the same level as dairy milk, i.e. 120 mg of calcium per 100 ml of milk.

CAN I LOSE WEIGHT BY FOLLOWING A SOYA-BASED DIET?

Most soya products are low in saturated fat and contain fibre, and their high protein content helps to control hunger pangs. However, you can only lose weight if you consume fewer calories than you expend in activity and exercise. You need to look at your whole diet and make sure it is balanced, low in saturated fat and high in fibre. You should also be eating five portions of fruit and vegetables a day.

IS SOYA SUITABLE FOR DAIRY ALLERGIES?

Most soya milk alternatives, textured vegetable protein and tofu will be dairy free. Ready-made products such as soya burgers, soya sausages and ready-meals using textured vegetable protein or tofu may contain dairy-based ingredients so it is important to read the packs carefully.

I'M LACTOSE INTOLERANT, CAN I USE SOYA PRODUCTS?

The same rules apply as for dairy allergies. Most milk, yogurt, cream and custard alternatives, as well as tofu, will be lactose free. However, products that contain textured vegetable protein, and ready-made dishes and meals, may have added lactose and it is always best to check the label. If you are following any diet that eliminates a specific food, it is always best to discuss this first with your doctor and registered dietitian, to ensure that your diet is properly balanced.

WHAT ABOUT SOYA ALLERGIES?

Soya allergies can occur, but they are extremely rare. If you are concerned about this, you should discuss it with your doctor or registered dietitian.

ARE SOYA PRODUCTS WHEAT- AND GLUTEN-FREE?

Most plain soya milk alternatives, tofu and textured vegetable protein will be wheat- and gluten-free. However, you need to check the label on all products, as there may be wheat derivatives among the added ingredients.

IS SOYA EXPENSIVE?

Textured vegetable protein is far cheaper than the meat equivalent and tofu is cheaper than a meat or cheese serving of the same size. Other soya dairy alternatives are roughly the same price as their dairy alternatives.

CAN SOYA CAUSE CANCER?

The consumption of whole soya foods such as soya milk alternatives, tofu and textured vegetable protein has not been shown to cause cancer. On the contrary, countries where large amounts of whole soya foods are consumed have much lower rates of breast and prostate cancer than Europe and the US.

HOW LONG CAN I STORE SOYA MILK, YOGURT, CREAM AND CUSTARD ALTERNATIVES FOR?

Unopened fresh, chilled soya milk alternatives and yogurts, as well as tofu, have a shelf life of around one month. Long-life products (such as milk alternatives and textured vegetable protein) have a long shelf-life (up to as much as nine months). Once opened, however, the product should generally be consumed within three to five days. All products vary, however, and it is therefore important to check the pack for best-before dates, as well as for recommendations on how to store the product once the packet is opened.

CAN I USE SOYA MILK INSTEAD OF DAIRY MILK?

Generally you can, yes. Soya milk can be used in tea, on cereal and in cooking, as you would use dairy milk. However, you may need to adapt the recipes slightly. Soya milk has a tendency to curdle, however, and will do so if it is poured straight into coffee or tea, so heat and whisk the milk first, as you would for cappuccinos and lattes.

WHAT ABOUT SOYA BEANS AND GMO?

Most soya beans from the US are genetically modified. However, beans sourced from outside the US are less likely to be GM. The only way to find out is to check the packaging – all products containing GMOs have to be clearly labelled.

IS QUORN MADE FROM SOYA?

No, this is a common misconception. Quorn™ is a vegetarian alternative to meat, and is made from a fungus that's a member of the mushroom family.

start the day

Fruity Summer Milkshake

Preparation time 2 minutes

Makes 2 x 300 ml (½ pint) glasses

1 ripe peach, halved, stoned and chopped

150 g (5 oz) strawberries

150 g (5 oz) raspberries

200 ml (7 fl oz) soya milk

ice cubes

NUTRITIONAL VALUES
89 kcals
5 g protein (3 g soya protein)
2.3 g fat
0.4 g saturated fat
4 g fibre

You can use any mixture of soft summer fruits in this recipe, such as nectarines, redcurrants or blackberries. Depending how sweet the fruit is, you might need to add a little extra honey. For a richer flavour, try substituting 100 ml (3½ fl oz) soya cream for the same quantity of soya milk.

1 Put the peach in a blender or food processor with the strawberries and raspberries and blend to a smooth purée, scraping the mixture down from the sides of the bowl if necessary.

2 Add the soya milk and blend the ingredients again until the mixture is smooth and frothy. Pour the milkshake over the ice cubes in tall glasses.

Silken Mango Smoothie

Preparation time 5 minutes

Makes 2 x 300 ml (½ pint) glasses

Silken tofu blends to a smooth, creamy texture that is perfect for blending with fresh fruits. Store the ingredients in the fridge before preparing if you like your smoothies chilled.

125 g (4 oz) silken tofu

1 large banana

½ large mango, skinned, stoned
  and cut into chunks

juice of 2 large oranges

1 tablespoon clear honey

mango wedges, to decorate (optional)

NUTRITIONAL VALUES
228 kcals
6 g protein (5 g soya protein)
1.8 g fat
0.3 g saturated fat
5.2 g fibre
Good source of phytoestrogens

1 Put the tofu, banana and mango in a blender or food processor, and blend to a smooth purée, scraping the mixture down from the sides of the bowl, if necessary.

2 Add the orange juice and honey and blend again until smooth. Pour into tall glasses and serve decorated with the mango wedges, if using.

Creamy Hot Chocolate

Like all the best hot chocolate drinks, this one is made by melting good-quality chocolate in milk and whisking it to get a frothy dose of warming comfort food.

Preparation time 2 minutes

Cooking time 3 minutes

Makes 2 mugs

1 Put the chocolate and soya milk in a small, heavy-based pan and heat very gently until the chocolate has melted, stirring frequently, until smooth and creamy.

2 Whisk to give the chocolate a frothy topping. (Use a hand-held electric immersion blender, if you have one.)

3 Pour the hot chocolate into mugs, sprinkle with cocoa powder and serve immediately.

125 g (4 oz) plain or milk chocolate, chopped

400 ml (14 fl oz) soya milk

cocoa powder, for sprinkling

NUTRITIONAL VALUES
430 kcals
11 g protein (6 g soya protein)
24 g fat
12 g saturated fat
1 g fibre
Good source of phytoestrogens

Nutty Passion Fruit Yogurts

Once made, these will keep in the fridge for up to two days. If clementines are unavailable, use other citrus fruits such as pink grapefruit or red-fleshed oranges.

Preparation time 5 minutes

Serves 2

1 Halve the passion fruit and scoop the pulp into a large bowl. Add the yogurt and mix them together gently.

2 Put two tablespoonfuls of the honey in the bases of 2 narrow glasses and scatter with half of the hazelnuts. Spoon half of the yogurt over the nuts and arrange half of the clementine pieces on top of the yogurt.

3 Repeat the layering, reserving a few of the nuts for decoration. Scatter the nuts over the top and chill the yogurts until you are ready to serve them.

2 passion fruit

250 ml (8 fl oz) natural soya yogurt

4 tablespoons clear honey

50 g (2 oz) hazelnuts, toasted and roughly chopped

4 clementines, peeled and chopped into small pieces

NUTRITIONAL VALUES
348 kcals
11 g protein (6 g soya protein)
21 g fat
1.9 g saturated fat
4 g fibre
Good source of phytoestrogens

Creamy Blueberry Porridge

Preparation time 5 minutes, plus overnight soaking

Cooking time 20 minutes

Serves 2

65 g (2½ oz) medium oatmeal

1 tablespoon honey

pinch of salt

400 ml (14 fl oz) soya milk

40 g (1½ oz) semi-dried blueberries

50 g (2 oz) no-soak apricots, roughly chopped

2 tablespoons pumpkin seeds

2 teaspoons demerara sugar

NUTRITIONAL VALUES
440 kcals
15 g protein (6 g soya protein)
14 g fat
1.7 g saturated fat
6 g fibre
Good source of phytoestrogens

Soaking oatmeal overnight in milk gives it an invitingly creamy texture, and means the dish is ready to cook quickly in the morning. Semi-dried blueberries and apricots make a colourful topping but most other semi-dried fruits could be used instead.

1 Put the oatmeal, honey, salt and soya milk in a large bowl and stir thoroughly to combine them. Cover the mixture and chill it in the fridge overnight.

2 Tip the mixture into a large pan and bring almost to the boil, watching so that it doesn't boil over. Reduce the heat and cook the porridge very gently for 15–20 minutes, until it is thickened and smooth, stirring frequently. (Alternatively cook the porridge in a large bowl in the microwave, on medium power, for 4–5 minutes, stirring twice.)

3 In a small bowl, mix together the semi-dried fruit, pumpkin seeds and sugar. Turn the porridge into serving bowls and scatter the fruit mixture over the top.

Luxury Fruit and Nut Muesli

Preparation time 5 minutes

Serves 2

Soya milk gives this tasty muesli a creamier flavour than apple juice. You could make up a larger batch of the dry ingredients to last several days, adding the yogurt mixture, fresh fruit and juice or milk just before serving.

50 g (2 oz) porridge oats

25 g (1 oz) unblanched almonds, toasted and roughly chopped

25 g (1 oz) brazil nuts, toasted and chopped

2 tablespoons sunflower seeds

50 g (2 oz) raisins

1 red apple or pear, cored, quartered and chopped

150 ml (¼ pint) natural soya yogurt

1 tablespoon honey, plus extra for serving

½ teaspoon vanilla extract

200 ml (7 fl oz) apple juice or soya milk

NUTRITIONAL VALUES

551 kcals

18 g protein (7 g soya protein with soya milk, 4 g soya protein without soya milk)

30 g fat

4 g saturated fat

6 g fibre

Good source of phytoestrogens, with use of soya milk

1 Put the oats, nuts, sunflower seeds and raisins in a large bowl. Add the apple or pear to the bowl and mix the ingredients together, until evenly distributed.

2 In a small bowl, mix together the soya yogurt, honey and vanilla extract until they are well combined.

3 Turn the muesli into cereal bowls and stir in the apple juice or soya milk. Serve topped with the vanilla yogurt and drizzle with extra honey.

Grilled Tofu Toast with Muscovado Figs

Set yourself up for the day with this invigorating blend of fruit, grainy bread and smooth silken tofu. The star anise – a pretty, star-shaped spice often used in Chinese cuisine – will add an aniseed flavour.

Preparation time 5 minutes

Cooking time 10 minutes

Serves 2

1 Put the sugar in a small, heavy-based pan with the star anise and water. Heat gently until the sugar has dissolved, then bring the mixture to the boil and boil rapidly for 3 minutes until it is reduced and syrupy.

2 Toast the bread on one side under a hot preheated grill. Cut the figs into quarters.

3 Spread the silken tofu onto the untoasted sides of the bread and arrange the fig quarters on top. Drizzle with 2 tablespoons of the syrup, then grill for 3–5 minutes, until the figs are beginning to colour. Transfer to plates and serve with the remaining syrup drizzled over.

4 tablespoons light muscovado sugar

3 star anise

150 ml (¼ pint) water

2 thick slices grainy bread

3 fresh figs

125 g (4 oz) silken tofu

NUTRITIONAL VALUES
293 kcals
10 g protein (5 g soya protein)
4 g fat
0.6 g saturated fat
3 g fibre
Good source of phytoestrogens

Cinnamon Tofu Toast with Poached Plums

Preparation time 10 minutes

Cooking time 10 minutes

Serves 2

A delicious, energy-building breakfast for when you have some time to spare. The poached plums can be made in larger quantities and kept in the fridge for several days. Serve chilled or warm.

400 g (13 oz) red plums, halved and stoned

50 g (2 oz) golden caster sugar, plus 4 teaspoons

100 ml (3½ fl oz) water

2 thick slices sweet bread, such as brioche or panettone

125 g (4 oz) tofu

¼ teaspoon ground cinnamon

NUTRITIONAL VALUES
329 kcals
9 g protein (5 g soya protein)
6 g fat
1 g saturated fat
3.2 g fibre
Good source of phytoestrogens

1 Put the plums in a heavy-based pan with the 50 g (2 oz) of sugar and the water. Heat gently, stirring, until the sugar has dissolved. Cover and simmer gently for 5 minutes, or until the plums have softened but are not falling apart.

2 Lightly toast the bread on one side, under a preheated hot grill. Pat the tofu dry on kitchen paper and cut into very thin slices. Arrange the slices over the untoasted sides of the bread. Mix together the remaining 4 teaspoons of sugar with the cinnamon, and sprinkle over the tofu. Cook under a moderate grill, watching closely, until the bread is toasted and the tofu begins to colour.

3 Spoon the poached plums and some of the cooking syrup into shallow serving bowls. Cut the toasts into triangles and serve with the plums.

Cranberry Muffins

Preparation time 10 minutes

Cooking time 20 minutes

Makes 12

Finely chopped stem ginger provides a sweet contrast to the tangy dried cranberries in these easy muffins. They are best eaten fresh.

150 g (5 oz) soya flour

150 g (5 oz) self-raising flour

1 tablespoon baking powder

65 g (2½ oz) light muscovado sugar

3 pieces stem ginger from a jar, about 50 g (2 oz), finely chopped

100 g (3½ oz) dried cranberries

1 egg

250 ml (8 fl oz) soya milk

4 tablespoons soya oil

NUTRITIONAL VALUES
172 kcals
7 g protein (5 g soya protein)
7.8 g fat
1.2 g saturated fat
2 g fibre
Good source of phytoestrogens

1 Line a 12-section muffin tray with paper muffin cases. Sift the flours and baking powder into a large bowl. Stir in the sugar, ginger and cranberries until evenly distributed.

2 In a separate bowl, beat together the egg, milk and oil, then add the liquid to the flour mixture. Using a large metal spoon, gently stir the liquid into the flour, until only just combined. The mixture should look craggy, with specks of flour still visible.

3 Divide the mixture between the muffin cases, piling it up in the centre. Bake in a preheated oven, 200°C (400°F, Gas Mark 6), for 18–20 minutes, until well risen and golden. Transfer to a wire rack and serve while still slightly warm.

Vanilla Bean Muffins

The tiny black seeds of the vanilla bean (or pod) give real depth of flavour to these breakfast muffins.

Preparation time 10 minutes

Cooking time 20 minutes

Makes 12

1 Line a 12-section muffin tray with paper muffin cases. Split the vanilla pod lengthways, using the tip of a sharp knife, and place in a small pan with 100 ml (3½ fl oz) of the milk. Bring just to the boil then remove from the heat and leave to cool slightly. Remove the vanilla pod from the pan and scoop out the seeds with a teaspoon. Stir them into the milk and discard the pod.

2 Sift the flour and baking powder into a large bowl, then stir in the sugar. In a separate bowl, beat together the eggs, soya oil, yogurt, vanilla milk and remaining soya milk. Using a large metal spoon, gently stir the liquid into the flour until only just combined.

3 Divide the mixture between the muffin cases and bake in a preheated oven, 200°C (400°F, Gas Mark 6), for about 20 minutes, until well risen and golden. Transfer to a wire rack and dust with icing sugar. Serve slightly warm.

1 vanilla pod

200 ml (7 fl oz) soya milk

325 g (11 oz) self-raising flour

1 tablespoon baking powder

125 g (4 oz) caster sugar

2 eggs

4 tablespoons soya oil

200 ml (7 fl oz) natural soya yogurt

icing sugar, for dusting

NUTRITIONAL VALUES
198 kcals
5 g protein (1.3 g soya protein)
6 g fat
1.2 g saturated fat
0.8 g fibre

Sweet Crêpes with Papaya Yogurt

A lovely breakfast treat for a leisurely morning. The crêpes can be made ahead and chilled overnight or frozen, interleaved with squares of greaseproof paper.

Preparation time 20 minutes

Cooking time 15 minutes

Serves 4

1 large papaya

4 tablespoons lime juice

5 tablespoons light muscovado sugar

100 g (3½ oz) plain flour

1 egg

300 ml (½ pint) soya milk

3 tablespoons soya oil, for frying

150 ml (¼ pint) natural soya yogurt

NUTRITIONAL VALUES
342 kcals
7.7 g protein (2.2 g soya protein)
12.4 g fat
2.1 g saturated fat
3.9 g fibre

1 Halve the papaya and scoop out the seeds. Cut away the skin and thinly slice the flesh. Put the slices in a bowl with the lime juice and 4 tablespoons of the sugar. Stir together and leave for 10 minutes so the sugar dissolves to make a syrupy sauce.

2 Put the flour in a separate bowl with the remaining sugar. Make a well in the centre and add the egg and a little of the soya milk. Whisk together, gradually incorporating the flour, to make a smooth batter. Whisk in the remaining soya milk.

3 Heat a little of the oil in a medium crêpe pan, or frying pan, and drain off the excess. When the pan is very hot, pour in a little of the batter, tilting the pan so the batter coats the base. Cook over a moderate heat until the batter is golden on the underside. Turn the crêpe over and cook for a further 30 seconds. Slide the crêpe out of the pan and keep it warm while you cook the remainder, lightly oiling the pan each time.

4 Fold the crêpes into quarters on serving plates, allowing two per portion. Top with the soya yogurt, papaya and syrup.

Herby Eggs with Smoked Salmon

Preparation time 5 minutes

Cooking time 3 minutes

Serves 2

Keep a pack of silken tofu in the cupboard for this energy-building breakfast, which makes a good kick-start for a busy day.

150 g (5 oz) silken tofu

3 eggs

15 g (½ oz) soya spread

4 tablespoons soya milk

3 tablespoons chopped herbs such as tarragon, chives, parsley and fennel, plus extra leaves to decorate

75 g (3 oz) smoked salmon, cut into strips

2 slices grainy bread, toasted

salt and pepper

NUTRITIONAL VALUES
407 kcals
32 g protein (7.2 g soya protein)
24 g fat
5 g saturated fat
1.6 g fibre
Good source of phytoestrogens

1 Put the tofu in a large bowl and break up into small pieces using a fork. Add the eggs and a little seasoning and beat again.

2 Melt the soya spread in a small, heavy-based pan and add the milk and beaten egg mixture. Cook over a gentle heat, stirring with a wooden spoon, until lightly scrambled.

3 Stir the herbs and smoked salmon into the pan and season with plenty of black pepper. Transfer the toast to warmed serving plates and spoon the scrambled eggs over it. Decorate with a few herb leaves.

light lunches

Mackerel Pâté with Fresh Soda Bread

Preparation time 20 minutes

Cooking time 20 minutes

Serves 4

200 ml (7 fl oz) soya milk, plus extra
   for brushing

2 teaspoons lemon juice

100 g (3½ oz) soya flour

125 g (4 oz) self-raising flour

2 teaspoons baking powder

¼ teaspoon salt

2 spring onions, finely chopped

3 tablespoons freshly chopped herbs

2 tablespoons olive oil

250 g (8 oz) smoked mackerel,
   skinned

1 tablespoon hot horseradish sauce

100 ml (3½ fl oz) natural soya yogurt

butter, for greasing

NUTRITIONAL VALUES
534 kcals
27 g protein (17 g soya protein)
34 g fat
6 g saturated fat
4 g fibre
Good source of phytoestrogens

Freshly baked yeast-free breads can be made in minutes and taste just as good as traditional ones. If you do not use it at once, warm it through before serving for a better flavour and texture.

1 Lightly grease a baking sheet. In a bowl, mix together the milk and lemon juice. Sift the flours, baking powder and salt into a separate large bowl.

2 Stir the spring onions, herbs and olive oil into the milk mixture. (The lemon juice will have thickened and slightly curdled the milk.) Add this to the flours and mix together to form a firm dough.

3 Tip out onto a lightly floured surface and shape into a long 'baguette'. Transfer to the baking sheet, brush with a little extra milk and score diagonally with a sharp knife. Bake in a preheated oven, 220°C (425°F, Gas Mark 7), for about 20 minutes, until risen and pale golden. Transfer to a wire rack to cool.

4 For the pâté, check over the mackerel for any bones and flake it into a blender or food processor. Add the horseradish sauce and yogurt and blend to a thick paste, scraping the mixture down from the sides of the bowl. Turn into a small serving dish and serve with the warm bread.

Sun-Blush Bruschetta

Even slightly stale bread can be put to good use in this simple lunch-time snack. Any leftover topping will keep well in the fridge for a couple of days.

Preparation time 10 minutes

Cooking time 5 minutes

Serves 2

1 Heat 1 tablespoon of the oil in a small frying pan and fry the onion gently for 3 minutes until softened.

2 Pat the tofu dry on kitchen paper and crumble it into the pan. Add the tomatoes, pesto and a little salt and pepper to the pan and stir them over a gentle heat for 2 minutes, until hot.

3 Mix the remaining oil with the garlic. Toast the bread on both sides and brush with the garlic oil. Pile the tofu mixture on top and serve sprinkled with basil leaves.

2 tablespoons olive oil

½ small red onion, finely chopped

125 g (4 oz) tofu

50 g (2 oz) sun-blush tomatoes, chopped

3 tablespoons pesto

1 small garlic clove, crushed

4 chunky slices country bread or ciabatta

small handful of basil leaves

salt and pepper

NUTRITIONAL VALUES
647 kcals
20 g protein (5.1 g soya protein)
46 g fat
9 g saturated fat
1.3 g fibre
Good source of phytoestrogens

Spicy Pitta Pockets with Mint Yogurt

Preparation time 15 minutes

Cooking time 5 minutes

Serves 4

Toasted pitta breads make handy containers for this lunchtime snack. It is ideal for lunch when you want something tasty and quick.

1 bunch spring onions, finely chopped

1 garlic clove, crushed

1 red chilli, deseeded and chopped

1 teaspoon cumin seeds, crushed

1 teaspoon caster sugar

4 tablespoons sesame seeds

250 g (8 oz) tofu

1 egg

100 ml (3½ fl oz) natural soya yogurt

2 tablespoons finely chopped mint

2 tablespoons soya oil, for frying

handful of salad leaves

4 pitta breads, split and toasted

salt

NUTRITIONAL VALUES
312 kcals
14 g protein (6.3 g soya protein)
18 g fat
2.9 g saturated fat
2 g fibre

1 Reserve 1 tablespoon of the chopped spring onions and put the remainder in a food processor with the garlic, chilli, cumin seeds, sugar and 2 tablespoons of the sesame seeds. Pat the tofu dry on kitchen paper and crumble it into the food processor. Blend it to a chunky paste, scraping the mixture down from the sides of the bowl if necessary.

2 Blend in the egg and a little salt. Divide the mixture into 8 portions and shape each into a flat cake in the palms of your hands. Coat both sides lightly with the remaining sesame seeds.

3 In a small bowl, mix together the reserved spring onions with the soya yogurt, mint and a little salt. Turn the mixture into a small serving dish.

4 Heat the oil in a large frying pan and fry the tofu cakes for 2 minutes on each side until golden. Pack a few salad leaves and 2 tofu cakes into each pitta and serve with the minty dressing.

Balsamic Marinated Tofu Panini

Tofu readily absorbs the strong flavours of marinades and dressings, as in this simple Italian sandwich.

Preparation time 5 minutes, plus marinating

Cooking time 6–8 minutes

Serves 2

1 Pat the tofu dry on kitchen paper and cut it into thin slices. Put these in a small bowl with the balsamic vinegar, rosemary and a little salt and pepper. Turn the tofu gently in the seasoned vinegar until coated, then leave to marinate for 30 minutes.

2 Halve the panini rolls and drizzle the cut sides with the olive oil. Arrange the tomato and tofu slices on the bread bases, drizzle with any excess vinegar and season with salt and pepper. Press the bread tops firmly down onto the filling.

3 Preheat a heavy-based frying pan or griddle and cook the panini for 3–4 minutes on each side, until deep golden. For a more traditional panini, weigh down the sandwiches using a small metal baking tray with heavy cans on to flatten the bread or use an electric sandwich maker. Serve the panini with watercress or rocket leaves.

125 g (4 oz) tofu

3 tablespoons balsamic vinegar

1 teaspoon finely chopped rosemary

2 panini rolls

3 tablespoons extra virgin olive oil

2 plum tomatoes, thinly sliced

watercress or rocket leaves, to serve

salt and pepper

NUTRITIONAL VALUES
368 kcals
12 g protein (5 g soya protein)
21 g fat
3 g saturated fat
2 g fibre
Good source of phytoestrogens

Gingered Tofu and Mango Salad

Fresh, ripe mango slices provide plenty of sweet contrast to the spicy sauce in this colourful salad. It is perfect for any lunch.

Preparation time 15 minutes, plus marinating

Cooking time 5 minutes

Serves 2

1 Pat the tofu dry on kitchen paper and cut into 1-cm (½-inch) cubes. In a small bowl, mix together the ginger, soy sauce, garlic and vinegar. Add the tofu to the bowl and toss the ingredients together. Set aside to marinate for 15 minutes.

2 Lift the tofu from the marinade with a fork, drain it and reserve the marinade. Heat the oil in a frying pan and gently fry the tofu pieces for about 3 minutes until golden. Drain and keep them warm. Add the spring onions and cashews to the pan and fry quickly for 30 seconds. Add the mango slices to the pan and cook for 30 seconds, until heated through.

3 Pile the shredded lettuce onto serving plates and scatter the tofu, spring onions, mango and cashew nuts over the top. Heat the marinade juices in the pan with the water, pour the mixture over the salad and serve immediately.

125 g (4 oz) tofu

25 g (1 oz) fresh root ginger, grated

2 tablespoons light soy sauce

1 garlic clove, crushed

1 tablespoon seasoned rice vinegar

2 tablespoons groundnut or soya oil

1 bunch spring onions, sliced diagonally into 2-cm (¾-inch) lengths

40 g (1½ oz) cashew nuts

1 small mango, halved, stoned and sliced

½ small iceberg lettuce, shredded

2 tablespoons water

NUTRITIONAL VALUES
340 kcals
11 g protein (5 g soya protein)
24 g fat
4 g saturated fat
4 g fibre
Good source of phytoestrogens

Tomato, Tofu and Hot Pepper Salad

Preparation time 10 minutes

Serves 2

Use any canned or bottled peppers to add plenty of sweetness and bite to this salad, but make sure they're not too fiery. Serve with grainy bread for mopping up the juices.

1 large beefsteak tomato, thinly sliced

125 g (4 oz) tofu

50 g (2 oz) hot piquante peppers, drained and thinly sliced

3 tablespoons snipped chives

2 tablespoons chopped flat leaf parsley

50 g (2 oz) pine nuts, toasted

40 g (1½ oz) sultanas

4 tablespoons olive oil

2 tablespoons lemon juice

2 teaspoons caster sugar

salt and pepper

NUTRITIONAL VALUES
527 kcals
11 g protein (5 g soya protein)
43 g fat
5 g saturated fat
2 g fibre
Good source of phytoestrogens

1 Arrange the tomato slices on two serving plates, lightly seasoning the layers with salt and pepper. Crumble the tofu into a mixing bowl then add the peppers, chives, parsley, pine nuts and sultanas and mix together.

2 In a small jug or bowl, whisk together the olive oil, lemon juice and sugar. Season lightly with salt and pepper and mix into the salad. Spoon the salad over the sliced tomatoes.

Citrus Chicken Salad with Beans

Preparation time 15 minutes

Cooking time 40 minutes

Serves 4

This summery salad is best served chilled, so you can cook the beans and chicken a day in advance, ready for last-minute assembly.

2 skinned, boned chicken breast fillets

1 teaspoon finely grated orange rind, plus 4 tablespoons juice

150 g (5 oz) mangetout, shredded lengthways

250 g (8 oz) cooked soya beans (see page 19)

125 g (4 oz) bean sprouts

½ cucumber, halved lengthways and sliced

2 tablespoons clear honey

4 tablespoons tahini

2 tablespoons lemon juice

2 tablespoons olive oil

salt and pepper

NUTRITIONAL VALUES
464 kcals
40 g protein (13 g soya protein)
27 g fat
4 g saturated fat
8 g fibre
Good source of phytoestrogens

1 Arrange the chicken fillets on a large piece of foil. Mix the orange rind with 1 tablespoon of the orange juice, season with salt and pepper and brush over the chicken. Bring the foil up over the chicken, sealing it into a parcel, and bake it on a baking tray in a preheated oven, 180°C (350°F, Gas Mark 4), for 40 minutes, or until the chicken is cooked through. Leave it to cool.

2 Shred the cooled chicken into pieces. Bring a pan of water to the boil and cook the mangetout for 1 minute, then drain them. Mix the mangetout, chicken, cooked beans, bean sprouts and cucumber together in a large bowl.

3 Mix the remaining orange juice with the honey, tahini, lemon juice and olive oil. Season with salt and pepper and add to the mixture in the bowl. Toss the salad well before serving.

Flageolet, Anchovy and Tofu Salad

Flageolets are tiny French green beans that are available in cans. They work well in this salad, complementing the other flavours.

Preparation time 10 minutes, plus chilling

Cooking time 5 minutes

Serves 4

1 Pat the tofu dry on kitchen paper. Cut into 1-cm (½-inch) chunks and season with salt and pepper. Heat 1 tablespoon of the oil in a frying pan and gently fry the tofu, stirring frequently, for 5 minutes, until the tofu is golden.

2 Tip the tofu into a bowl and add the beans, garlic, anchovies, onion and herbs. Mix together gently to combine.

3 Mix the vinegar, mustard and the rest of the oil together with a little pepper and add to the bowl. Toss the ingredients together, then cover and chill for at least 1 hour. Serve with grainy bread to mop up the juice.

250 g (8 oz) tofu

5 tablespoons extra virgin olive oil

1 x 400 g (13 oz) can flageolet beans, drained and rinsed

2 garlic cloves, thinly sliced

6 anchovy fillets, finely sliced

½ small red onion, finely sliced

2 tablespoons chopped flat leaf parsley

1 teaspoon chopped rosemary

3 tablespoons balsamic vinegar

1 teaspoon grainy mustard

salt and pepper

NUTRITIONAL VALUES
350 kcals
16 g protein (5 g soya protein)
19 g fat
2 g saturated fat
1 g fibre
Good source of phytoestrogens

Pancetta, Mushroom and Bean Soup

Preparation time 10 minutes

Cooking time 30 minutes

Serves 2–3

The intense flavour of the pancetta – an Italian unsmoked bacon – gives this hearty winter bean soup a real bite.

2 tablespoons olive oil

100 g (3½ oz) cubed pancetta

1 onion, finely chopped

2 garlic cloves, crushed

100 g (3½ oz) button mushrooms, sliced

275 g (9 oz) cooked soya beans (see page 19)

3 tablespoons sun-dried tomato paste

900 ml (1½ pints) chicken stock

1 tablespoon chopped oregano

1 tablespoon chopped flat leaf parsley, plus extra to garnish

salt and pepper

natural soya yogurt, to serve

NUTRITIONAL VALUES
401 kcals
21 g protein (13 g soya protein)
29 g fat
6 g saturated fat
8 g fibre
Good source of phytoestrogens

1 Heat the oil in a large pan and fry the pancetta for 3 minutes, until lightly browned. Add the onion to the pan and fry gently for 5 minutes. Add the garlic and mushrooms and continue to fry for a further minute.

2 Tip the soya beans into the pan with the sun-dried tomato paste, stock and herbs. Bring to the boil. Reduce the heat, cover the pan and simmer the soup very gently for 20 minutes.

3 Check the seasoning and ladle into soup bowls. Serve topped with swirls of yogurt and scattered with extra parsley.

Creamy Corn and Asparagus Chowder

Preparation time 10 minutes

Cooking time 30 minutes

Serves 2–3

This soup is chunky, full of flavour and substantial. If you prefer, you could either blend it roughly with an electric immersion blender or process it in a food processor until it is velvety smooth.

225 g (1 oz) butter

1 large onion, finely chopped

2 celery sticks, sliced

300 ml (½ pint) vegetable stock

500 g (1 lb) new potatoes, cut into
    small chunks

2 teaspoons finely chopped rosemary

600 ml (1 pint) soya milk

250 g (8 oz) baby corn, cut diagonally
    into thin slices

250 g (8 oz) asparagus, cut diagonally
    into thin slices

freshly grated nutmeg, to garnish

salt and pepper

NUTRITIONAL VALUES
235 kcals
11 g protein (4 g soya protein)
10 g fat
4 g saturated fat
5 g fibre

1 Melt the butter in a large pan. Add the onion and fry gently for 3 minutes. Add the celery and fry for a further 2 minutes.

2 Add the stock, potatoes and rosemary to the pan and bring to the boil. Reduce the heat, cover, and simmer gently for 10 minutes, until the potatoes are tender.

3 Add the soya milk to the pan and bring it almost to the boil. Reduce the heat to a gentle simmer and add the corn and asparagus. Cook gently for about 5 minutes, until the vegetables are tender. Season with salt and pepper to taste and grate plenty of nutmeg into each soup bowl before serving.

Miso Broth with Vegetable Noodles

In Japan, miso soup is eaten any time of the day, even for breakfast. Its salty, spicy flavour might suit our palettes better for lunch. Dashi is available from Asian supermarkets but you could use a fish or vegetable stock instead.

Preparation time 10 minutes

Cooking time 8 minutes

Serves 2

1 In a large pan, blend the dashi powder with the water. Heat until it is almost boiling, then reduce the heat to a gentle simmer. Add the spring onions, sugarsnaps and mushrooms to the pan and cook gently for 2 minutes.

2 In a cup, blend the miso paste with a little of the hot stock, and pour it back into the soup. Add the tofu and noodles to the soup and cook gently for about 4 minutes, until the noodles are tender. Serve hot.

2 teaspoons dashi

750 ml (1¼ pints) water

4 spring onions, finely sliced

100 g (3½ oz) sugarsnap peas, shredded diagonally

50 g (2 oz) shiitake mushrooms

2 tablespoons miso paste

100 g (3½ oz) silken tofu, diced

40 g (1½ oz) fine rice noodles

NUTRITIONAL VALUES
245 kcals
12 g protein (7 g soya protein)
4 g fat
0.3 g saturated fat
1 g fibre
Good source of phytoestrogens

Roasted Red Peppers with Tapenade

Tapenade is easy to make and its strong, garlicky flavour is perfect for livening up the mild-tasting tofu. This is a great make-ahead veggie lunch if you bake and fill the peppers in advance, ready for reheating.

Preparation time 20 minutes

Cooking time 45 minutes

Serves 4

4 red peppers, halved and deseeded

3 tablespoons extra virgin olive oil

100 g (3½ oz) pitted black olives

2 garlic cloves, roughly chopped

1 tablespoon chopped oregano

4 tablespoons sun-dried tomato paste

250 g (8 oz) tofu

200 g (7 oz) cherry tomatoes, halved

chopped fresh parsley, to serve

salt and pepper

NUTRITIONAL VALUES
332 kcals
8 g protein (5 g soya protein)
28 g fat
4 g saturated fat
4 g fibre
Good source of phytoestrogens

1 Put the peppers, cut sides up, in a roasting tin, drizzle with 1 tablespoon of the oil and season with salt and pepper. Roast in a preheated oven, 200°C (400°F, Gas Mark 6), for 25–30 minutes, until lightly browned.

2 To make the tapenade, put the olives, garlic, oregano, tomato paste and the remaining olive oil in a food processor or blender. Blend to a thick paste, scraping down the mixture from the sides of the bowl.

3 Pat the tofu dry on kitchen paper and cut into 1-cm (½-inch) dice. Toss in a bowl with the tapenade. Pile the mixture into the peppers, with the cherry tomatoes, and return to the oven for a further 15 minutes, until the tomatoes have softened and the filling is hot.

4 Transfer to serving plates and scatter liberally with plenty of chopped fresh parsley.

Tofu and Pesto Frittata

This deep, Italian-style omelette is lovely served warm, with a tomato or leafy salad, or cold as a snack the following day.

Preparation time 10 minutes

Cooking time 25–30 minutes

Serves 2–3

1 large potato, about 250 g (8 oz), thinly sliced

4 eggs

2 tablespoons soya milk

250 g (8 oz) tofu

3 tablespoons green or red pesto

3 tablespoons olive oil

2 small onions, chopped

salt and pepper

basil leaves, to garnish

NUTRITIONAL VALUES
61 kcals
21 g protein (7 g soya protein)
33 g fat
8 g saturated fat
2 g fibre
Good source of phytoestrogen

1 Cook the potato in plenty of lightly salted boiling water for 3 minutes, or until just tender. Drain in a colander. In a bowl, beat together the eggs and milk, and season lightly with salt and pepper.

2 Pat the tofu dry on kitchen paper and cut in half. Cut each half horizontally into very thin slices and spread the top of each slice with pesto.

3 Heat the oil in a medium, heavy-based frying pan and fry the onions for 8–10 minutes, or until deep golden. Remove half the onions, spread the remainder out in the pan and scatter half the potato slices over the top. Arrange half the tofu slices over the potato then add a second layer of the potatoes and tofu and finally the rest of the onions.

4 Pour the egg mixture into the pan and return to the heat on its lowest setting. Cook very gently for about 10 minutes, until the eggs are lightly set. Place the pan under a preheated moderate grill and cook for a further 3–5 minutes, or until the surface is pale golden. Serve scattered with basil leaves.

Spicy Soya Couscous

Harissa is a Moroccan chilli paste and is traditionally served with couscous. You will find it in jars in the supermarket.

Preparation time 20 minutes

Cooking time 40 minutes

Serves 4

1 Heat the oil in a large pan and gently fry the onion, carrots and celery for about 10 minutes, until the onions are golden. Add the garlic, cinnamon and cumin seeds to the pan and fry them gently for 2 minutes.

2 Add the tomatoes, harissa paste, sugar and cooked beans and cover. Cook the mixture gently for 25 minutes, or until the vegetables are just tender.

3 Meanwhile, using the boiling water, prepare the couscous with the boiling water according to the instructions on the packet. (Different types of couscous require slightly different methods.)

4 Fluff up the couscous with a fork and transfer it to serving plates. Stir the coriander into the sauce and season with salt and pepper to taste. Ladle the sauce over the couscous and serve.

3 tablespoons olive oil

1 large onion, chopped

200 g (7 oz) carrots, thinly sliced

4 celery sticks, sliced

3 garlic cloves, crushed

2 cinnamon sticks

2 teaspoons cumin seeds

2 x 400 g (13 oz) cans chopped tomatoes

2 teaspoons harissa paste

2 teaspoons dark muscovado sugar

300 g (10 oz) cooked soya beans (see page 19)

350 ml (12 fl oz) boiling water

300 g (10 oz) couscous

25 g (1 oz) fresh coriander, chopped

salt and pepper

NUTRITIONAL VALUES
435 kcals
18 g protein (11 g soya protein)
15 g fat
1.9 g saturated fat
8 g fibre
Good source of phytoestrogens

Stir-Fried Tofu with Prawns

Preparation time 10 minutes

Cooking time 10 minutes

Serves 2

250 g (8 oz) tofu

3 tablespoons soy sauce

1 tablespoon clear honey

1 tablespoon soya or groundnut oil

150 g (5 oz) spring greens, shredded

300 g (10 oz) cooked rice noodles

200 g (7 oz) cooked, peeled prawns

4 tablespoons hoisin sauce

2 tablespoons chopped fresh coriander

NUTRITIONAL VALUES
390 kcals
39 g fat
12.7 g fat
1.8 g saturated fat
2.2 g fibre
Good source of phytoestrogens

Stir-frying is one of the best ways to cook tofu, particularly when it has been marinated in soy sauce for extra flavour. Pre-packed, ready-cooked noodles make a perfect partner, cutting down on cooking time and saucepans.

1 Pat the tofu dry on kitchen paper and cut into 2-cm (¾-inch) dice. Mix the soy sauce and honey together in a small bowl, then add the tofu and mix gently. Leave to stand for 5 minutes.

2 Drain the tofu, reserving the marinade, and pat the cubes dry on kitchen paper. Heat the oil in a large frying pan and fry the tofu for 5 minutes, stirring, until it is crisp and golden. Drain the pieces and keep them warm.

3 Add the greens to the pan and fry them quickly, stirring, until they are wilted. Return the tofu to the pan with the noodles and prawns and cook them briskly, tossing the ingredients together, for 2 minutes.

4 Mix the hoisin sauce with the reserved marinade. Drizzle the liquid over the stir-fry, mix it in, scatter over the fresh coriander and serve immediately.

Spicy Tofu Burgers with Cucumber Relish

Preparation time 15 minutes

Cooking time 15 minutes

Serves 4

Red kidney beans add colour and texture to these chunky burgers, but other cooked beans, such as soya beans, would work in this dish just as well.

4 tablespoons soya or groundnut oil

1 small red onion, finely chopped

1 celery stick, finely chopped

2 garlic cloves, crushed

1 x 220 g (7 oz) can red kidney beans

75 g (3 oz) salted peanuts

250 g (8 oz) tofu

2 teaspoons medium curry paste

50 g (2 oz) breadcrumbs

1 egg

½ small cucumber, peeled and deseeded

2 tablespoons chopped flat leaf parsley

1 tablespoon white wine vinegar

2 teaspoons caster sugar

NUTRITIONAL VALUES
417 kcals
19 g protein (5 g soya protein)
26 g fat
4 g saturated fat
6 g fibre
Good source of phytoestrogens

1 Heat 1 tablespoon of the oil in a frying pan and gently fry all but 1 tablespoon of the onion with the celery for 5 minutes until they are soft. Add the garlic and fry for a further 2 minutes.

2 Put the kidney beans in a bowl and mash them lightly with a fork to break them up. Finely chop the peanuts in a food processor. Pat the tofu dry on kitchen paper, break it into pieces and add it to the nuts in the food processor. Blend them until the tofu is crumbly then add the mixture to the beans together with the fried vegetables, curry paste, breadcrumbs and egg, and mix everything well to obtain a thick paste.

3 Divide the mixture in the bowl into quarters and shape into burgers, dusting your hands with floud if the mixture is sticky. Heat the remaining oil in the pan and gently fry the burgers for about 4 minutes on each side, until golden.

4 Meanwhile, chop the cucumber finely and mix it with the reserved tablespoon of chopped onion, the parsley, vinegar and sugar in a small bowl. Serve with the burgers.

Asian Tofu Steaks

Preparation time 15 minutes, plus marinating

Cooking time 10 minutes

Serves 4

Chunky pieces of tofu seep up the strong flavours of garlic, soy sauce and wasabi, a hot paste made from Japanese horseradish. If no wasabi is available, use horseradish sauce.

250 g (8 oz) tofu

3 garlic cloves, crushed

4 tablespoons light soy sauce

2 teaspoons wasabi paste

4 teaspoons light muscovado sugar

300 g (10 oz) pak choi, quartered lengthways

250 g (8 oz) wide rice noodles

2 tablespoons groundnut or soya oil

25 g (1 oz) fresh coriander, roughly chopped

2 tablespoons lime juice

2 tablespoons sesame oil

100 ml (3½ fl oz) chicken or vegetable stock

1 tablespoon sesame seeds, toasted

NUTRITIONAL VALUES
440 kcals
10 g protein (5 g soya protein)
18 g fat
2 g saturated fat
1.2 g fibre

1 Pat the tofu dry on kitchen paper. Cut it into four squares and slice each square horizontally into two chunky steaks. Put these in a shallow bowl. Mix together the garlic, soy sauce, wasabi paste and sugar and pour them over the tofu. Cover the tofu and set it aside to marinate for 30 minutes.

2 Bring a large pan of water to the boil and blanch the pak choi for 1 minute. Drain it and then cook the noodles according to the instructions on the packet.

3 Heat the groundnut or soya oil in a large frying pan. Lift the tofu steaks from the marinade, drain them and reserve the marinade. Fry the tofu for 2 minutes on each side, until it is a deep golden colour. Drain and keep warm.

4 Add the pak choi to the pan and fry for 1 minute. Add the drained noodles, coriander, lime juice, sesame oil, stock and marinade juices to the pan. Heat through gently for 1 minute, tossing the ingredients together. Transfer to serving plates, scatter with the sesame seeds and top with the tofu steaks.

Smoky Tofu Pizza

Don't be put off by the idea of making the pizza base, it's very easy and makes such a difference to the finished result. If you prefer, use plain tofu instead of smoked.

Preparation time 20 minutes, plus proving

Cooking time 25 minutes

Serves 3–4

1 Put the flour, salt, yeast and 2 tablespoons of the oil in a mixing bowl and stir in the water. Mix to a dough, adding a little more water if the dough feels dry. Turn out onto a lightly floured surface and knead for 5 minutes until smooth. Place in a lightly oiled bowl, cover with cling film and leave to rise in a warm place for about 45 minutes, until it has doubled in size.

2 Lightly oil a large baking sheet. Turn the risen dough onto a floured surface and roll out to a 30-cm (12-inch) round. Transfer to the baking sheet.

3 Heat the remaining oil in a frying pan and fry the onions for 5 minutes, or until they are soft. Tip the tomatoes into a sieve and stir them to drain off some of the juice. Mix the pulp in a bowl with the sun-dried tomato paste and season with salt and pepper. Spread to within 1.5 cm (¾ inch) of the edges of the dough. Pat the tofu dry on kitchen paper and cut it into thin slices. Scatter these over the dough with the pepperoni slices, fried onions and cheese. Sprinkle with the oregano.

4 Bake in a preheated oven, 220°C (425°F, Gas Mark 7), for 15–20 minutes, until the pizza crust is golden and the cheese melting.

275 g (9 oz) strong white bread flour, plus extra for dusting

½ teaspoon salt

1 teaspoon easy-blend dried yeast

3 tablespoons olive oil

175 ml (6 fl oz) hand-hot water

2 small red onions, thinly sliced

1 x 220 g (7 oz) can chopped tomatoes

3 tablespoons sun-dried tomato paste

220 g (7½ oz) smoked tofu

50 g (2 oz) pepperoni, thinly sliced

100 g (3½ oz) pecorino Romano or Parmesan cheese, grated

½ teaspoon dried oregano

salt and pepper

NUTRITIONAL VALUES
588 kcals
26 g protein (5 g soya protein)
30 g fat
10 g saturated fat
3 g fibre
Good source of phytoestrogens

Lemony Bean and Bacon Penne

A quick and easy lunch dish that needs only a simple leaf salad to accompany it. Lightly mashing the cooked soya beans helps them to absorb all the lemony butter juices.

Preparation time 5 minutes

Cooking time 20 minutes

Serves 2

1 Lightly mash the soya beans in a bowl with a fork. Bring a large pan of lightly salted water to the boil and cook the pasta, according to instructions on the packet, until it is tender.

2 Meanwhile, heat the oil in a large frying pan and fry the bacon and onion for about 6–8 minutes, until golden. Stir in the mashed beans and rosemary and cook gently for 2 minutes until the mixture is heated right through. Lightly drain the pasta and add it to the pan.

3 Mix the lemon juice and butter in the pan. Season the sauce with salt and pepper and heat gently, stirring, until the butter has melted. Serve the pasta immediately.

100 g (3½ oz) cooked soya beans (see page 19)

125 g (4 oz) penne pasta

2 tablespoons olive oil

100 g (3½ oz) back bacon, chopped

1 onion, chopped

2 teaspoons chopped rosemary

2 tablespoons lemon juice

25 g (1 oz) butter

salt and pepper

NUTRITIONAL VALUES
632 kcals
24 g protein (7 g soya protein)
35 g fat
12 g saturated fat
7 g fibre
Good source of phytoestrogens

Devilled Tofu and Mushrooms

Preparation time 10 minutes

Cooking time 12 minutes

Serves 2

Use a really chunky, grainy bread for the toast so that it absorbs all the sweet and spicy devilled sauce.

½ teaspoon cornflour

juice of 1 large orange

2 tablespoons mango chutney

2 tablespoons Worcestershire sauce

1 tablespoon grainy mustard

125 g (4 oz) tofu

40 g (1½ oz) butter

375 g (12 oz) large open mushrooms

2 chunky slices wholegrain bread,
   toasted

salt

NUTRITIONAL VALUES
433 kcals
14 g protein (5 g soya protein)
22 g fat
12 g saturated fat
6 g fibre
Good source of phytoestrogens

1 Blend the cornflour with a little of the orange juice in a small bowl until smooth. Add the chutney to the ingredients in the bowl, chopping up any large pieces, together with the Worcestershire sauce, mustard and the remaining orange juice.

2 Pat the tofu dry on kitchen paper and cut it into 1-cm (½-inch) dice. Melt the butter in a frying pan and fry the tofu for 3–5 minutes, turning it frequently, until golden, then drain it. Fry the mushrooms in the pan for 5 minutes.

3 Return the tofu to the pan with the sauce and cook gently for 2 minutes, stirring, until the sauce is slightly thickened and bubbling. Season with salt and pepper and spoon it over the hot toast.

White Chocolate and Cardamom Mousse

Preparation time 10 minutes,
plus chilling

Serves 6–8

Silken tofu blends to a smooth paste in the food processor, making it an ideal base for sweet, creamy desserts. The cardamom adds a distinctive taste.

200 g (7 oz) white chocolate, chopped

4 tablespoons soya milk

12 cardamom pods

200 g (7 oz) silken tofu

50 g (2 oz) caster sugar

1 egg white

crème fraîche or soya yogurt, to serve

cocoa powder, for dusting

NUTRITIONAL VALUES
192 kcals
6 g protein (2 g soya protein)
10 g fat
5 g saturated fat
0 g fibre

1 Put the chocolate and soya milk in a heatproof bowl and leave to melt, over a saucepan of gently simmering water. To release the cardamom seeds, crush the pods using a pestle and mortar. Discard the pods and crush the seeds finely.

2 Put the tofu and cardamom seeds in a food processor with half of the sugar, and blend well to a smooth paste. Turn the mixture into a large bowl.

3 Whisk the egg white in a thoroughly clean bowl, until it forms peaks. Gradually whisk in the remaining sugar.

4 Beat the melted chocolate mixture into the tofu until completely combined. Using a large metal spoon, fold in the egg white. Spoon the mousse into small coffee cups or glasses and chill for at least 1 hour. Serve topped with spoonfuls of crème fraîche or soya yogurt and a light dusting of cocoa powder.

Aromatic Fruit Salad with Ginger

A little freshly grated ginger can be used to enhance the simplest fruit salad. The soya and mascarpone topping is also lovely spooned over hot sponge puddings and poached fruits.

Preparation time 15 minutes

Serves 6

1 Tip the ginger into a small pan with any juice. Add the sugar and water and heat gently until the sugar has dissolved. Bring to the boil and boil for 2 minutes. Leave to cool.

2 Scoop the passion fruit pulp into a large bowl. Mix in the other fruit. Strain the ginger syrup through a sieve and mix again. Cover and chill.

3 Beat the mascarpone in a bowl to soften it. Add the yogurt, lime rind and juice and icing sugar. Mix well. Transfer the fruit salad to serving bowls, spoon the mascarpone sauce over them and serve.

25 g (1 oz) piece of fresh root ginger, grated

25 g (1 oz) caster sugar

150 ml (¼ pint) water

4 passion fruit

1 medium pineapple, cored and chopped

3 large bananas, sliced

1 large papaya, halved, deseeded and chopped

300 g (10 oz) red grapes, halved

250 g (8 oz) mascarpone cheese

250 ml (8 fl oz) natural soya yogurt

finely grated rind of 1 lime, plus 2 teaspoons juice

3 tablespoons icing sugar

NUTRITIONAL VALUES
346 kcals
10 g protein (2 g soya protein)
12 g fat
6.3 g saturated fat
3 g fibre

Lemon Yogurt Ice

Preparation time 10 minutes, plus freezing

Cooking time 2 minutes

Serves 4

Serve this as a lighter, more refreshing alternative to ice cream or as a long, cooling summer drink, scooped into glasses and topped up with lemonade.

175 g (6 oz) caster sugar

150 ml (¼ pint) water

finely grated rind and juice of 2 large lemons

500 ml (17 fl oz) natural soya yogurt

NUTRITIONAL VALUES
262 kcals
6 g protein (6 g soya protein)
5 g fat
0.8 g saturated fat
0 g fibre
Good source of phytoestrogens

1 Put the sugar and water in a large pan and heat gently, stirring, until the sugar has dissolved. Leave to cool.

2 Whisk in the lemon rind, juice and yogurt until the mixture is very smooth.

3 To freeze by hand, pour the mixture into a shallow freezer container and freeze for 3–4 hours, until frozen around the edges and slushy in the centre. Turn it into a bowl and whisk with an electric whisk until it is smooth. Return it to the container and re-freeze, until softly frozen. Repeat the freezing and whisking process, until the yogurt ice has a creamy consistency.

4 To freeze using an ice-cream maker, churn until the mixture is thick and creamy then transfer to a freezer container and freeze.

5 Transfer the yogurt ice to the fridge to soften slightly about 30 minutes before serving.

hearty mains

Thai Tofu Cakes

Preparation time 20 minutes

Cooking time 12 minutes

Serves 4

Kaffir lime leaves are widely used in Thai cookery. They are sold dried and you should be able to find them in supermarkets. These cakes make a lovely light main course, served with a herb salad and fragrant rice.

1 bunch spring onions, roughly chopped

25 g (1 oz) piece of fresh root ginger, roughly chopped

1 lemon grass stalk, roughly chopped

4 garlic cloves, chopped

2 teaspoons caster sugar

2 teaspoons Thai fish sauce

2 kaffir lime leaves

250 g (8 oz) tofu

100 g (3½ oz) breadcrumbs

1 egg white

3 tablespoons groundnut or soya oil

2 tablespoons clear honey

1 tablespoon light soy sauce

1 tablespoon seasoned rice vinegar

1 red chilli, deseeded and finely chopped

NUTRITIONAL VALUES
258 kcals
10 g protein (9 g soya protein)
12 g fat
1.6 g saturated fat
1 g fibre
Good source of phytoestrogens

1 Put the spring onions, ginger, lemon grass, garlic, sugar and fish sauce in a food processor. Crumble the lime leaves, if using dried, or chop them if fresh, and add them to the processor. Blend the ingredients to a paste, scraping the mixture down from the sides of the bowl.

2 Pat the tofu dry on kitchen paper. Break it into pieces and add them to the spices together with the breadcrumbs. Blend the mixture until just combined then add the egg white and blend again.

3 Shape dessert spoonfuls of the mixture into flat cakes, lightly dusting your hands with a little flour if the mixture feels sticky.

4 Brush the tops of the cakes with a little oil and cook them in a large heavy-based frying pan, oiled sides down, for about 2 minutes, until golden. Brush the tops of the cakes with a little more oil, turn them over and cook for a further 1–2 minutes. Drain them and keep them warm while cooking the remainder.

5 Meanwhile, mix the honey, soy sauce, vinegar and chilli in a small bowl. Serve this dipping sauce with the tofu cakes.

Fragrant Pilaf

Preparation time 20 minutes

Cooking time 30 minutes

Serves 4

This is rather like an Indian biryani, made using tempeh instead of chicken or lamb. If tempeh is not available, use tofu, patted dry on kitchen paper, instead.

1 teaspoon saffron strands

3 onions

15 g (½ oz) piece of fresh root ginger, roughly chopped

4 garlic cloves, roughly chopped

2 teaspoons cumin seeds

½ teaspoon dried chilli flakes

5 tablespoons groundnut or soya oil

250 g (8 oz) tempeh

12 cardamom pods, lightly crushed

1 tablespoon black onion seeds

300 g (10 oz) basmati rice

600 ml (1 pint) vegetable stock

150 g (5 oz) French beans

150 g (5 oz) fresh or frozen peas

3 tablespoons raisins

3 tablespoons toasted flaked almonds

NUTRITIONAL VALUES
692 kcals
26 g protein (13 g soya protein)
22 g fat
2.5 g saturated fat
9 g fibre
Good source of phytoestrogens

1 Crumble the saffron into 1 tablespoon of boiling water and leave to stand. Thinly slice 2 of the onions and set them aside. Roughly chop the remaining onion and blend it to a paste in a food processor with the ginger, garlic, cumin, chilli and 2 tablespoons of cold water.

2 Heat 1 tablespoon of the oil in a large pan and fry the sliced onions for about 8 minutes until golden. Drain them and set them aside. Cut the tempeh into 1.5-cm (¾-inch) dice. Add another tablespoon of the oil to the pan and fry the tempeh for 5 minutes, until it is lightly coloured, then drain it. Add the cardamom and black onion seeds to the pan and fry them for a further 30 seconds.

3 Tip the paste and remaining oil into the pan and stir it in, until the juice evaporates. Stir in the rice and cook for 1 minute.

4 Add the stock and bring it to the boil. Reduce the heat, cover the pan and cook the rice very gently for 8–10 minutes, until it is tender and the stock absorbed. Add a little more stock if the rice becomes too dry.

5 Cut the French beans into 5-cm (2-inch) lengths. Stir in the saffron and its liquid, the peas, beans and tempeh into the rice and cook for 5 minutes. Turn onto warmed serving plates. Briefly reheat the fried onions and scatter over the pilaf with the raisins and toasted almonds.

Smoky Kedgeree

Smoked tofu has a more intense flavour than plain tofu and makes a delicious partner to egg and cheese dishes, or any dish that uses smoked fish or meat.

Preparation time 10 minutes

Cooking time 25 minutes

Serves 4

1 Pat the tofu dry on kitchen paper. Cut it into 2 x 1-cm (¾ x ½-inch) dice. Put the eggs in a small pan, cover them with cold water and bring it to the boil. Simmer gently for 4 minutes then drain and shell the eggs, then quarter them lengthways.

2 Cook the rice in plenty of boiling, lightly salted water for 10 minutes or until tender, then drain it.

3 Melt half of the butter in a large frying pan. Add the onion and fry gently, stirring, for 3 minutes or until this onion is just beginning to colour. Add the tofu and cook for a further 3 minutes or until both are golden. Stir the curry paste into the mixture, then add the cooked rice, eggs, lime rind and parsley and toss the ingredients together, over a gentle heat, until warmed through.

4 Dot the remaining butter over the rice and drizzle the lime juice over the top. Fold in gently and serve immediately with lime wedges.

220 g (7½ oz) smoked tofu

4 eggs

250 g (8 oz) basmati rice

50 g (2 oz) butter

1 onion, finely chopped

1 teaspoon curry paste

finely grated rind of 1 lime, plus
   1 tablespoon juice

3 tablespoons chopped flat leaf parsley

salt and pepper

lime wedges, to serve

NUTRITIONAL VALUES
484 kcals
18 g protein (5 g soya protein)
21 g fat
9 g saturated fat
1 g fibre
Good source of phytoestrogens

Cheese and Leek Risotto

This recipe is a super-fast version of a traditional risotto in which the liquid is added to the pan in one go. It means you do not have to stir the rice continuously, but do not leave the room altogether because it does cook very quickly.

Preparation time 10 minutes

Cooking time 25 minutes

Serves 4

450 ml (¾ pint) soya milk

450 ml (¾ pint) vegetable or chicken stock

2 medium leeks, about 300 g (10 oz)

50 g (2 oz) butter

300 g (10 oz) Arborio rice

2 garlic cloves, sliced

150 ml (¼ pint) white wine

125 g (4 oz) blue-veined cheese

salt and pepper

NUTRITIONAL VALUES
554 kcals
17 g protein (3 g soya protein)
24 g fat
13 g saturated fat
2 g fibre

1 Put the soya milk and stock in a medium pan and heat the liquid through gently. Trim the leeks, cut into quarters lengthways, then chop the lengths into thin slices.

2 Melt half of the butter in a large pan and sauté the leeks gently for 5 minutes, until they are softened. Add the rice and garlic and cook the risotto for a further minute, stirring continuously. Pour in the wine and let the mixture bubble, until the wine has almost totally evaporated.

3 Stir the warmed soya milk mixture into the rice. Cover the pan and simmer the risotto gently for 10–15 minutes, stirring occasionally until the rice is tender and creamy.

4 Crumble the cheese into the risotto and dot it with the remaining butter. Stir this in gently, season with a little salt and pepper and serve immediately.

Smoked Tofu and Apricot Sausages

Preparation time 20 minutes

Cooking time 10 minutes

Serves 4

This quantity makes 8 small sausages, so you might want to make double the quantity for people with larger appetites. Serve them with chunky chips and a spicy relish.

220 g (7½ oz) smoked tofu

2 tablespoons olive or soya oil, plus a little extra for frying

1 large onion, roughly chopped

2 celery sticks, roughly chopped

100 g (3½ oz) no-soak dried apricots, roughly chopped

50 g (2 oz) breadcrumbs

1 egg

1 tablespoon chopped sage

salt and pepper

NUTRITIONAL VALUES
232 kcals
10 g protein (5 g soya protein)
10 g fat
1.7 g saturated fat
3 g fibre
Good source of phytoestrogens

1 Pat the tofu dry on kitchen paper and tear into chunks. Heat the oil in a frying pan and fry the onion and celery for 5 minutes, until they are softened. Tip them into a food processor and add the tofu and apricots. Blend the ingredients to a chunky paste, scraping down the mixture from the sides of the bowl if necessary.

2 Tip the mixture into a mixing bowl and add the breadcrumbs, egg and sage. Season with salt and pepper and beat well until everything is evenly combined.

3 Divide the mixture into 8 portions. Using lightly floured hands, shape each portion into a sausage, pressing the mixture together firmly. Heat a little oil in a frying pan, preferably non-stick, and fry the sausages for about 5 minutes, until they are golden.

Chilli Tofu Kebabs

Preparation time 20 minutes,
  plus soaking

Cooking time 8 minutes

Serves 4

150 g (5 oz) bulgar wheat

250 g (8 oz) tofu

50 g (2 oz) breadcrumbs

3 rashers smoked bacon, finely chopped

2 garlic cloves, crushed

25 g (1 oz) fresh root ginger, grated

½ teaspoon dried chilli flakes

1 small red onion, finely chopped

10 large mint leaves, chopped

1 egg

2 tablespoons groundnut or soya oil

½ small ripe mango, stoned and
  finely chopped

2 teaspoons lime juice

100 ml (3½ fl oz) natural soya yogurt

leafy salad, to serve

salt

NUTRITIONAL VALUES
397 kcals
18 g protein (1 g soya protein)
15 g fat
3.1 g saturated fat
2 g fibre

These kebabs have a spicy Mediterranean flavour that is complemented by the refreshing and tasty mango yogurt.

1 Put the bulgar wheat in a bowl and cover it with plenty of boiling water. Leave it to stand for 30 minutes, until the bulgar wheat has softened and drain it thoroughly. Soak 8 wooden skewers in water while preparing the tofu.

2 Pat the tofu dry on kitchen paper. Put it in a food processor with the bulgar wheat and blend them to a thick paste. Tip the paste into a bowl and add the breadcrumbs, bacon, garlic, ginger, chilli, onion, mint and a little salt. Add the egg and beat the mixture well to make a thick, evenly combined paste.

3 Divide the paste into 8 even-sized balls. Thread a ball of paste onto each skewer and flatten it into a sausage shape. Brush with the oil.

4 Cook the skewers under a preheated moderate grill for about 6–8 minutes, turning once or twice, until the kebabs are turning golden. Mix the mango with the lime juice and yogurt in a small serving dish. Serve the chilli kebabs with crisp salad leaves and the mango yogurt.

Caesar Salad with Cheesy Tofu Croutons

Preparation time 10 minutes

Cooking time 10 minutes

Serves 4

Chunks of tofu roasted with Parmesan in a hot oven make crispy croutons with a lovely toasted cheese flavour that are perfect in this healthy take on a classic Caesar salad.

250 g (8 oz) tofu

100 g (3½ oz) Parmesan cheese, finely grated

6 tablespoons extra virgin olive oil

1 egg

1 garlic clove, crushed

2 teaspoons Dijon mustard

3 anchovy fillets, chopped

2 tablespoons lemon juice

1 Cos lettuce, shredded

salt and pepper

NUTRITIONAL VALUES

368 kcals

20 g protein (5 g soya protein)

31 g fat

8 g saturated fat

1 g fibre

Good source of phytoestrogens

1 Pat the tofu dry on kitchen paper and cut into 1-cm (½-inch) dice. Scatter in a roasting tin with 50 g (2 oz) of the Parmesan and 1 tablespoon of the oil. Cook in a preheated oven, 200°C (400°F), Gas Mark 6, for about 10 minutes, until the cheese is golden. Leave to cool for a couple of minutes then transfer to a plate, breaking up any brittle pieces of baked cheese.

2 Lower the egg into a small pan of boiling water and cook it for 2 minutes, then drain. Put the garlic, mustard, anchovy fillets and lemon juice in a food processor and blend them to a smooth paste. Gradually blend in the remaining oil. Carefully peel and halve the egg and scoop the very soft yolk and white into the dressing. Blend again, until smooth and the consistency of thin mayonnaise. Season with salt and pepper.

3 Shred the lettuce into a salad bowl and scatter the tofu croutons over the leaves. Pour the dressing all over the dish and sprinkle with the remaining Parmesan.

Shredded Pork and Bean Salad with Sage

Pork is the best meat to include in this sage-infused salad, but for an alternative you could fry a couple of thinly sliced chicken breast fillets along with the onion.

Preparation time 15 minutes

Cooking time 10 minutes

Serves 4

1 Cook the French beans in a little water for 2 minutes, until they are just tender, then drain them. Heat 3 tablespoons of the oil in a large frying pan and fry the sage leaves for about 20 seconds, until they frizzle and crisp. Drain them with a slotted spoon and set them aside on kitchen paper.

2 Add the onion to the pan and fry gently it for 3 minutes, until it has softened. Add the pork and garlic and cook, stirring, for 2 minutes, until the garlic is beginning to colour.

3 Tip all the beans into the pan with the lemon juice, sugar and remaining oil and reheat for 2–3 minutes, tossing the ingredients together. Season with salt and pepper, transfer to serving plates and scatter the sage leaves over the salad.

200 g (7 oz) French beans, halved

6 tablespoons olive oil

16 large sage leaves

1 large red onion, chopped

250 g (8 oz) cooked pork, roughly shredded

4 garlic cloves, thinly sliced

300 g (10 oz) cooked soya beans (see page 19)

2 tablespoons lemon juice

1 teaspoon caster sugar

salt and pepper

NUTRITIONAL VALUES
408 kcals
31 g protein (11 g soya protein)
26 g fat
4 g saturated fat
7 g fibre
Good source of phytoestrogens

Summer Salad with Balsamic Marinade

Preparation time 15 minutes

Cooking time 20 minutes

Serves 2

The quantities for this salad can easily be halved for a starter or increased for more servings. Accompany with some chunky warmed bread for mopping up the juices.

250 g (8 oz) tofu

3 tablespoons balsamic vinegar

300 g (10 oz) asparagus tips, trimmed

4 plum tomatoes, halved

4 tablespoons extra virgin olive oil

100 g (3½ oz) baby spinach leaves

100 g (3½ oz) thinly sliced salami

1 teaspoon grainy mustard

2 tablespoons water

50 g (2 oz) Parmesan cheese, pared into shavings

salt and pepper

NUTRITIONAL VALUES
711 kcals
38 g protein (10 g soya protein)
58 g fat
16 g saturated fat
6 g fibre
Good source of phytoestrogens

1 Pat the tofu dry on kitchen paper, and cut into quarters, then cut each piece horizontally into thin slices. Place the slices on a plate and pour the balsamic vinegar over them and set them aside to marinate while you are roasting the vegetables.

2 Scatter the asparagus and tomatoes into a roasting tin and drizzle 2 tablespoons of the oil over them and season them with salt and pepper. Cook in a preheated oven, 200°C (400°F, Gas Mark 6), for 15 minutes or until the asparagus is tender and lightly browned. Arrange the tofu slices on top, reserving the marinade, and return the roasting tin to the oven for 5 minutes.

3 Pile the spinach and salami onto warmed serving plates and top with the asparagus, tomatoes and tofu. Add the remaining oil and the marinade to the roasting pan with the mustard and water and season with salt and pepper. Heat through for 30 seconds and pour over the salad. Serve scattered with Parmesan shavings.

Chermoula Tofu with Roasted Vegetables

Chermoula is a Moroccan blend of herbs and spices that is often used to liven up baked chicken and fish but it works just as well with tofu. Serve this dish with lightly buttered new potatoes for a fresh, summery main course.

Preparation time 15 minutes

Cooking time 1 hour

Serves 4

1 Mix the coriander, garlic, cumin, lemon rind and chillies together with 1 tablespoon of the oil and a little salt in a small bowl to make the chermoula.

2 Pat the tofu dry on kitchen paper and cut it in half. Cut each half horizontally into thin slices. Spread the chermoula generously over the slices.

3 Scatter the vegetables in a roasting tin and drizzle with the remaining oil. Bake in a preheated oven, 200°C (400°F, Gas Mark 6), for about 45 minutes, until lightly browned, turning the ingredients once or twice during cooking.

4 Arrange the tofu slices over the vegetables, with the side spread with the chermoula uppermost, and bake for a further 10–15 minutes, until the tofu is lightly coloured.

25 g (1 oz) fresh coriander, finely chopped

3 garlic cloves, chopped

1 teaspoon cumin seeds, lightly crushed

finely grated rind of 1 lemon

½ teaspoon dried crushed chillies

4 tablespoons olive oil

250 g (8 oz) tofu

2 red onions, quartered

2 courgettes, thickly sliced

2 red peppers, deseeded and sliced

2 yellow peppers, deseeded and sliced

1 small aubergine, thickly sliced

salt

NUTRITIONAL VALUES
241 kcals
10 g protein (5 g soya protein)
15 g fat
2 g saturated fat
6 g fibre
Good source of phytoestrogens

Soya Bean Moussaka

Preparation time 25 minutes

Cooking time 1¼ hours

Serves 5–6

This delicious vegetarian dish is packed with healthy ingredients, but without compromising the flavour. The aubergines are grilled, rather than fried, so they don't absorb too much oil.

2 aubergines, about 450 g (14½ oz), thinly sliced

4 tablespoons olive oil

2 onions, chopped

2 celery sticks, chopped

3 garlic cloves, crushed

1 teaspoon dried oregano

325 g (11 oz) cooked soya beans (see page 19)

2 x 400 g (13 oz) cans chopped tomatoes

4 tablespoons sun-dried tomato paste

250 ml (8 fl oz) natural soya yogurt

1 egg

75 g (3 oz) Cheddar or Gruyère cheese, grated

salt and pepper

NUTRITIONAL VALUES
346 kcals
17 g protein (9.7 g soya protein)
26 g fat fat
5.8 g saturated fat
6.1 g fibre
Good source of phytoestrogens

1 Line a large grill rack with foil. Arrange the aubergine slices in a single layer on the grill rack. Brush them with 3 tablespoons of the oil and season them with salt and pepper. Grill them for about 5 minutes, until they are pale golden, then turn the slices over and cook for a further 5 minutes.

2 Heat the remaining oil in a pan and gently fry the onions and celery for 5 minutes. Add the garlic, oregano, soya beans, tomatoes and tomato paste, season with salt and pepper and bring to the boil. Reduce the heat and simmer the sauce gently for about 15 minutes, until it is thick and pulpy.

3 Turn half of the sauce into a shallow ovenproof dish and arrange half of the aubergine slices on top. Spread with the remaining sauce over the top and add the rest of the aubergine slices in a layer.

4 Beat the yogurt, egg and half of the cheese together in a bowl and spoon the mixture over the dish. Sprinkle the remaining cheese over the top and bake the moussaka in a preheated oven, 180°C (350°F, Gas Mark 4), for about 45 minutes, until the surface is golden. Leave the moussaka to stand for 10 minutes before serving.

Chunky Squash Stew

Pieces of cooked ham from a large joint are ideal for this nourishing stew. Alternatively, buy a couple of small gammon steaks and add them to the stew, with the celery and carrots.

Preparation time 20 minutes

Cooking time 35 minutes

Serves 4

1 Halve the squash and discard the seeds. Cut away the skin and cut the flesh into chunky pieces. Melt the butter in a large pan and gently fry the onion for 3 minutes. Add the celery, carrots and squash to the pan and fry for a further 2 minutes.

2 Add the soya beans, stock and thyme and bring to the boil. Reduce the heat, stir in the ham and simmer gently, covered, for 20 minutes, until the vegetables are tender.

3 Meanwhile, sift the flour and baking powder into a bowl. Pat the tofu dry on kitchen paper and grate it into the bowl. Add the suet. Mix the mustard with the water and add to the bowl. Mix to a soft dough.

4 Stir the peas into the stew. Divide the dough into quarters in the bowl and spoon each quarter into the stew. Cover the pan and cook the stew gently for 10 minutes, or until the dumplings are risen and fluffy.

1 butternut squash, about 750 g (1½ lb)

25 g (1 oz) butter

1 large onion, chopped

2 celery sticks, sliced

2 carrots, sliced

200 g (7 oz) cooked soya beans (see page 19)

750 ml (1¼ pints) ham stock

several thyme sprigs

200 g (7 oz) ham, cut into small chunks

125 g (4 oz) self-raising flour

1 teaspoon baking powder

125 g (4 oz) tofu

50 g (2 oz) vegetable suet

2 teaspoons grainy mustard

150 ml (¼ pint) water

100 g (3½ oz) fresh or frozen peas

NUTRITIONAL VALUES
583 kcals
27 g protein (7 g soya protein)
31 g fat
15 g saturated fat
10 g fibre
Good source of phytoestrogens

Tempeh Balti

This curry is deliciously thick and spicy and because it contains potato, it's really a meal in itself. If you'd like a mild accompaniment, serve some plain or pilau basmati rice.

Preparation time 20 minutes

Cooking time 30 minutes

Serves 4

250 g (8 oz) tempeh

25 g (1 oz) fresh root ginger, grated

3 garlic cloves, crushed

2 onions, roughly chopped

6 cardamom pods

2 teaspoons each of cumin and coriander seeds

3 tablespoons groundnut or soya oil

2 cinnamon sticks and 2 bay leaves

6 whole cloves

1 red chilli, deseeded and chopped

½ teaspoon turmeric

2 x 400 g (13 oz) cans chopped tomatoes

2 teaspoons caster sugar

500 g (1 lb) potatoes, cut into cubes

225 g (7½ oz) spinach

NUTRITIONAL VALUES
376 kcals
20 g protein (13 g soya protein)
14 g fat
1.4 g saturated fat
9 g fibre
Good source of phytoestrogens

1 Cut the tempeh into 1-cm (½-inch) dice and mix in a bowl, with the ginger and garlic.

2 Blend the onions and 2 tablespoons of water to a purée in a food processor, scraping down the onions from the sides of the bowl if necessary. Lightly crush the cardamom pods with the cumin and coriander using a pestle and mortar.

3 Heat the oil in a large pan and fry the crushed spices with the cinnamon, bay leaves and cloves for 30 seconds. Tip the onion purée into the pan and add the chilli and turmeric. Cook, stirring, for 1 minute, then add the tomatoes, sugar and potatoes to the pan and cover. Simmer gently for 20 minutes, until the potatoes are tender and the sauce is thick. Add the tempeh and cook for a further 5 minutes.

4 Add the spinach to the pan, stirring it into the sauce, until it starts to wilt. Cook for a further 2 minutes, until the spinach is soft and coated in the spicy sauce.

Spicy Spanish Chorizo Hotpot

Chorizo sausage makes a great addition to stews. Its warm spicy flavour penetrates all the ingredients it is cooked with, particularly the tofu, which absorbs flavours like a sponge.

Preparation time 15 minutes, plus overnight soaking

Cooking time about 1½ hours

Serves 4

1 Put the drained beans in a large pan, cover with plenty of cold water and bring to the boil. Boil rapidly for 10 minutes, then reduce the heat and simmer gently for about 30 minutes, or until the beans are tender. Drain.

2 Pat the tofu dry on kitchen paper. Cut the tofu into 1-cm (½-inch) dice. Heat the oil in a large pan then add the chorizo and fry gently for 5 minutes, until lightly browned. Remove the chorizo from the pan with a slotted spoon then fry the tofu in the pan for 5 minutes, until the onions are golden. Drain the tofu then fry the onions and red peppers for 5 minutes, until golden. Add the celery and fry for a further 2 minutes.

3 Return the chorizo to the pan with the paprika, tomatoes, tomato paste, stock and beans. Bring to the boil, cover, and cook gently for 20 minutes. Add the tofu and cook for a further 5 minutes, until it is heated through.

200 g (7 oz) black beans, soaked overnight and drained

250 g (8 oz) tofu

4 tablespoons olive oil

200 g (7 oz) piece of chorizo sausage, cut into 1-cm (½-inch) dice

2 onions, sliced

2 red peppers, deseeded and sliced

2 celery sticks, sliced

2 teaspoons smoked paprika

1 x 400 g (13 oz) can chopped tomatoes

4 tablespoons sun-dried tomato paste

300 ml (½ pint) vegetable stock

NUTRITIONAL VALUES
422 kcals
19 g protein (5 g soya protein)
24 g fat
4 g saturated fat
6 g fibre
Good source of phytoestrogens

Chicken Fillets with Sweet Soy Glaze

Preparation time 10 minutes, plus chilling

Cooking time 30 minutes

Serves 4

This quick and easy supper dish could not be easier to prepare. Marinate the chicken in the soy mixture in the morning, so it is all ready to pop in the oven after work. Serve with steamed vegetables and rice or noodles.

4 chicken breast fillets, skinned

4 tablespoons dark soy sauce

3 tablespoons light muscovado sugar

2 garlic cloves, crushed

2 tablespoons white wine vinegar

100 ml (3½ fl oz) freshly squeezed orange juice

pepper

NUTRITIONAL VALUES
308 kcals
40 g protein (0 g soya protein)
8.4 g fat g fat
1.2 g saturated fat
0 g fibre

1 Lay the chicken fillets on a chopping board and slice each in half horizontally. Place in a large, shallow ovenproof dish, in which the fillets fit snugly.

2 Mix together the soy sauce, sugar, garlic, vinegar, orange juice and pepper and pour the mixture over the chicken. Cover and chill the dish until you are ready to cook it.

3 Uncover the dish and bake the chicken in a preheated oven, 180°C (350°F, Gas Mark 4), for 30 minutes, until it is cooked through. Transfer to serving plates and spoon the cooking juices over the meat.

Pan-fried Tuna with Miso Glaze

Preparation time 15 minutes

Cooking time 15 minutes

Serves 4

Rich miso paste flavoured with garlic, honey and ginger makes a sweet, glossy sauce for serving with firm, meaty fish like fresh tuna.

3 tablespoons groundnut or soya oil

1 bunch spring onions, sliced diagonally

150g (5oz) mangetout, halved lengthways

2 courgettes, cut into matchstick lengths

4 tuna steaks

2 garlic cloves, crushed

25g (1oz) fresh root ginger, grated

2 tablespoons miso paste

3 tablespoons clear honey

1 tablespoon rich soy sauce

100 ml (3½ fl oz) water

long grain rice, to serve

NUTRITIONAL VALUES
423 kcals
34 g protein (0 g soya protein)
11 g fat
1.9 g saturated fat
1.7 g fibre

1 Heat 2 tablespoons of the oil in a large frying pan and fry the spring onions, mangetout and courgettes for 4–5 minutes until they are softened, then drain them and keep them warm. Add the tuna steaks to the pan with the remaining oil and fry gently for about 4 minutes on each side until they are deep golden. Drain the steaks and keep them warm.

2 Add the garlic to the pan and fry gently for 30 seconds. Stir in the ginger, miso paste, honey, soy sauce and the water. Cook the glaze, stirring it continuously, until it is bubbling.

3 Pile the stir-fried vegetables over rice on warmed serving plates and arrange the tuna steaks on top. Pour the miso glaze over the fish and serve immediately.

Fennel and Monkfish Pie

Even small quantities of soya, in this case soya milk, can provide plenty of extra nutrients in your daily diet.

Preparation time 25 minutes

Cooking time 1 hour 5 minutes

Serves 4

1 Bring a large pan of salted water to the boil. Cook the potatoes for 3 minutes until they are softened, then drain them.

2 Melt half of the butter in a large frying pan and fry the fennel and onion for 10 minutes, until they are softened. Set the vegetables aside. Melt 15 g (½ oz) of the butter in the pan, add the monkfish and garlic, season lightly and fry for 3 minutes, turning the fish. Drain the fish using a slotted spoon.

3 Melt the remaining butter in the pan and stir in the flour. Take the pan off the heat and blend in the milk. Return the sauce to the heat and cook it, stirring, until it is bubbling and thinly coats the back of the spoon. Stir in half of the Gruyère and season the sauce.

4 Scatter half of the potato slices into a shallow pie dish and arrange the fish and vegetables over the top. Sprinkle with the herbs and pour half the sauce over them. Arrange the remaining potato slices on top and top with the rest of the sauce.

5 Sprinkle with the remaining Gruyère and bake in a preheated oven, 180°C (350°F, Gas Mark 4), for 45 minutes, until the surface is golden.

700 g (1 lb 7 oz) potatoes, cut into 5 mm (¼ inch) slices

50 g (2 oz) butter

2 fennel bulbs, trimmed and thinly sliced

1 small onion, finely chopped

350 g (12 oz) monkfish, cut into slices

2 garlic cloves, crushed

2 tablespoons plain flour

500 ml (1 pint) soya milk

100 g (3½ oz) Gruyère cheese, grated

4 tablespoons chopped mixed herbs such as parsley, fennel and tarragon

salt and pepper

NUTRITIONAL VALUES
502 kcals
31 g protein (4 g soya protein)
22 g fat
13 g saturated fat
4 g fibre

Salmon with Bean and Celeriac Mash

Preparation time 15 minutes

Cooking time 20 minutes

Serves 4

The blend of puréed soya beans, celeriac and potatoes is really delicious in this smooth and creamy mash. As an alternative to the salmon, try cod or haddock, or even steak or chicken.

250 g (8 oz) cooked soya beans (see page 19)

3 tablespoons water

1 medium celeriac, about 500 g (1 lb)

500 g (1 lb) potatoes, cut into chunks

4 salmon fillets

50 g (2 oz) butter

3 tablespoons chopped chives

3 tablespoons chopped tarragon or dill

1 tablespoon white wine vinegar

salt and pepper

NUTRITIONAL VALUES
479 kcals
29 g protein (9 g soya protein)
29 g fat
12 g saturated fat
10 g fibre
Good source of phytoestrogens

1 Put the cooked beans and water in a food processor and blend them to a smooth paste. Cut away the skin from the celeriac, cut the flesh into chunks and cook them in a pan of lightly salted boiling water, with the potatoes, for about 15 minutes, until tender.

2 Meanwhile, pat the salmon dry on kitchen paper and season it with salt and pepper. Heat 15 g (½ oz) of the butter in a frying pan and fry the salmon for 4–5 minutes on each side, until it is cooked through.

3 Drain the vegetables and return them to the pan with the blended beans and a further 15 g (½ oz) of the butter. Using a potato masher, mash the ingredients together until evenly combined. Reheat for 1–2 minutes and season with salt and pepper.

4 Pile the mash onto warmed serving plates and top with the salmon fillets. Add the remaining butter, herbs and vinegar to the frying pan and heat through until the mixture bubbles. Pour the sauce over the salmon and serve immediately.

Fish Laksa

The combination of prawns and noodles in an aromatic, spicy coconut broth is absolutely delicious and perfect for any occasion. Smaller bowlfuls make an equally good starter.

Preparation time 10 minutes

Cooking time 25 minutes

Serves 4

1 Put the chilli, lemon grass, onion, ginger and fish sauce in a food processor and blend them to a paste, scraping the mixture down from the sides of the bowl if necessary.

2 Heat the oil in a large, heavy-based pan, add the paste and turmeric and fry them gently, stirring, for 5 minutes. Add the fish stock and coconut milk and bring the mixture to the boil. Stir in the beans, reduce the heat and cook the broth gently for 15 minutes.

3 Meanwhile, cook the noodles according to the instructions on the packet. Drain the noodles and add to the broth with the prawns. Cook it gently for 2 minutes.

4 Add the bean sprouts and coriander and cook the laksa for a further minute, stirring, until heated through, then serve it in shallow bowls.

1 red chilli, deseeded and roughly chopped

1 lemon grass stalk, roughly chopped

1 large onion, roughly chopped

40 g (1½ oz) piece of fresh root ginger, peeled and sliced

4 teaspoons Thai fish sauce

3 tablespoons groundnut or soya oil

½ teaspoon ground turmeric

600 ml (1 pint) fish stock

1 x 400 ml (14 fl oz) can coconut milk

250 g (8 oz) cooked soya beans (see page 19)

250 g (8 oz) dried egg noodles

300 g (10 oz) raw or cooked peeled prawns

100 g (3½ oz) bean sprouts

4 tablespoons chopped fresh coriander

NUTRITIONAL VALUES
569 kcals
37 g protein (9 g soya protein)
20 g fat
4 g saturated fat
7 g fibre
Good source of phytoestrogens

Seared Scallops with Coriander Yogurt

Plump, juicy scallops make a fabulous main course treat, or you could serve smaller portions as an appetising starter.

Preparation time 15 minutes

Cooking time 5 minutes

Serves 2

150 ml (¼ pint) natural soya yogurt

2 tablespoons chopped fresh coriander

finely grated rind and juice of 1 lime

2 teaspoons sesame oil

½ small red onion, finely chopped

15 g (½ oz) fresh root ginger, grated

1 garlic clove, crushed

2 teaspoons caster sugar

2 teaspoons dark soy sauce

1 tablespoon water

1 pointed green pepper, thinly sliced

12 large scallops

rocket leaves, to serve

NUTRITIONAL VALUES
217 kcals
22 g protein (3.8 g soya protein)
7.6 g fat
1.3 g saturated fat
1.7 g fibre

1 In a small bowl, mix together the yogurt, coriander and lime rind, then transfer to a serving dish.

2 Heat half of the oil in a small pan and gently fry the onion for 3 minutes, until it has softened. Remove the pan from the heat and add the ginger, garlic, sugar, soy sauce, water and lime juice.

3 Brush a griddle with the remaining oil. Add the green pepper and scallops, cook the scallops for 1 minute on each side, until cooked through, and the pepper for a little longer, if necessary.

4 Pile the pepper and scallops onto serving plates with the rocket leaves. Heat the soy glaze through and spoon it over the scallops. Serve with the yogurt sauce.

Frozen Toffee Marble Cream

Preparation time 20 minutes, plus freezing

Cooking time 10 minutes

Serves 6

This toffee-swirled dessert is deliciously creamy, but without the richness of a traditional ice cream. For a dairy-free version, use a bought toffee sauce.

6 egg yolks

75 g (3 oz) caster sugar

6 teaspoons cornflour

900 ml (1½ pints) soya milk

2 teaspoons vanilla extract

175 g (6 oz) can evaporated milk

75 g (3 oz) muscovado sugar

NUTRITIONAL VALUES
237 kcals
10 g protein (4 g soya protein)
11 g fat
3.7 g saturated fat
0.0 g fibre

1 Whisk the egg yolks, caster sugar and 4 teaspoons of cornflour together in a bowl. Bring 600 ml (1 pint) of soya milk just to the boil in a heavy-based pan, then gradually whisk it into the egg-yolk mixture. Tip this custard into the pan and cook it over a very gentle heat, stirring, until it is thickened and smooth. Turn it into a bowl and stir in the vanilla extract and remaining soya milk. Leave it to cool.

2 Put the remaining cornflour in a small, heavy-based pan with a little evaporated milk and blend them to a smooth paste. Add the remaining evaporated milk and the sugar and cook over a gentle heat stirring until the sugar has dissolved. Increase the heat and stir the mixture until it is bubbling and thickly coating the back of the spoon. Remove the pan from the heat and leave the sauce to cool.

3 To make the ice cream, freeze the custard for about 4 hours until it is frozen around the edges. Turn the custard into a bowl and beat with an electric whisk until smooth. Repeat the process twice more, then whisk the ice cream again until it is thick and softly set. Return to the freezer container and drizzle the toffee sauce over it. Fold the two together with a dessert spoon to obtain a marbled effect. Re-freeze until firm and transfer to the fridge about 30 minutes before serving.

Honey and Ginger Ice Cream

Soya cream is a far healthier alternative to dairy cream in frozen desserts. This ice cream is lovely served on its own or you could melt it over hot puddings, fruit pies or crêpes.

Preparation time 15 minutes, plus freezing

Cooking time 5 minutes

Serves 6

1 Put the soya milk in a medium pan and bring it to the boil. Whisk the honey, egg yolks and cornflour together in a bowl until smooth. Whisk in the boiled milk and return the custard to the pan. Cook it over a very gentle heat, stirring, until it is slightly thickened. Transfer it to a bowl, cover it with a circle of greaseproof paper and leave it to cool.

2 Once the custard has cooled completely, stir in the soya cream and stem ginger.

3 To freeze by hand, pour the mixture into a shallow freezer container and freeze it for 3–4 hours, until solid around the edges and slushy in the centre. Whisk it in a bowl with an electric whisk until it is smooth. Return it to the container and re-freeze until it is softly frozen. Repeat the freezing and whisking procedure once or twice more, until the ice cream is smooth and creamy.

4 To freeze the ice cream using an ice-cream maker, churn the mixture until it is thick and creamy then transfer it to a freezer container and freeze it until you need it. Transfer the ice cream to the fridge 30 minutes before serving.

300 ml (½ pint) soya milk

125 g (4 oz) orange blossom honey

6 egg yolks

1 teaspoon cornflour

500 ml (17 fl oz) soya cream

65 g (2½ oz) stem ginger pieces, finely chopped

NUTRITIONAL VALUES
296 kcals
7.1 g protein (4 g soya protein)
21.4 g fat
4 g saturated fat
0.3 g fibre

Baked Cheesecake with Boozy Berries

Preparation time 20 minutes

Cooking time 40 minutes

Serves 8

Blackberries macerated in sugar and spirits develop a syrupy tang that is lovely against the creamy flavour of the cheesecake.

300 g (10 oz) blackberries

4 tablespoons gin or vodka

3 tablespoons icing sugar, plus extra for dusting

150 g (5 oz) digestive biscuits

50 g (2 oz) unsalted butter

250 g (8 oz) tofu

1 tablespoon cornflour

100 g (3½ oz) caster sugar

250 g (8 oz) cream cheese

2 eggs

150 ml (¼ pint) double cream

NUTRITIONAL VALUES
440 kcals
11 g protein (3 g soya protein)
28 g fat
16 g saturated fat
2 g fibre

1 In a bowl, mix together the blackberries, spirits and icing sugar. Cover and chill the fruit while you prepare the cheesecake.

2 Crush the biscuits in a polythene bag with a rolling pin. Melt the butter in a medium pan, then add the biscuits. Mix them together well and pack them into the base of a lightly greased 20-cm (8-inch) springform tin.

3 Pat the tofu dry on kitchen paper and break it into pieces in a food processor. Add the cornflour and caster sugar and blend the ingredients until smooth, scraping the mixture down from the sides of the bowl. Beat the cream cheese in a bowl until it is smooth. Beat the tofu paste and eggs into the cheese. Stir in the cream and pour the mixture into the biscuit-lined tin.

4 Bake in a preheated oven, 190°C (375°F, Gas Mark 5), for 40 minutes, until the surface is set but the centre of the cheesecake is still wobbly when the tin is shaken. Leave it to cool in the oven.

5 Transfer the cheesecake to a serving plate, dust it with icing sugar and serve it with the macerated berries.

Baked Apple Pud with Ginger Custard

Preparation time 20 minutes

Cooking time 45 minutes

Serves 4–5

Tofu can be discreetly added to the most traditional pudding. Sweet and buttery, this is comfort food at its best.

750 g (1½ lb) cooking apples, peeled, cored, quartered and sliced

200 g (7 oz) caster sugar

125 g (4 oz) tofu

125 g (4 oz) unsalted butter, softened, plus extra for greasing

2 eggs

100 g (3½ oz) self-raising flour

½ teaspoon baking powder

25 g (1 oz) piece of fresh root ginger, finely grated

2 egg yolks

25 g (1 oz) caster sugar

1 teaspoon cornflour

300 ml (½ pint) soya milk

NUTRITIONAL VALUES
585 kcals
11 g protein (4 g soya protein)
28 g fat
16 g saturated fat
3 g fibre

1 Place the apple slices inside a buttered, shallow ovenproof dish. Sprinkle with 75 g (3 oz) of sugar and 4 tablespoons of water.

2 Pat the tofu dry on kitchen paper and break it into pieces. Put these in a food processor with the butter and remaining sugar and blend until the mixture is smooth. Add the eggs, flour and baking powder and blend until the ingredients are evenly combined.

3 Turn the mixture out onto the apples and spread it in an even layer. Bake the pudding in a preheated oven, 180°C (350°F, Gas Mark 4), for about 45 minutes, until it is risen and deep golden.

4 Meanwhile, make the ginger custard. Whisk the ginger and its juices, the egg yolks, sugar and cornflour together in a bowl.

5 Bring the soya milk to the boil in a medium, heavy-based pan. Pour it over the ginger mixture, stirring well, then strain the custard through a sieve into the pan. Heat it very gently, stirring, until it thickly coats the back of the spoon. Pour the custard into a jug and serve it with the warm pudding.

Banana and Maple Syrup Cake

Serve this delicious sponge as a dessert when it is freshly cooked, or as a cake with tea or coffee, when it is a little firmer.

Preparation time 20 minutes

Cooking time 30 minutes

Serves 8

1 Grease a 20-cm (8-inch) round cake tin and line the base with greaseproof paper. Break the bananas into a bowl, mash them with a fork and then stir in the maple syrup.

2 Whisk the sugar, lemon rind, soya spread, eggs and flour together until the mixture is smooth and creamy. Stir the mashed bananas into it. Turn this sponge mixture into the prepared tin and level the surface. Scatter the almonds over the top.

3 Bake the sponge in a preheated oven, 180°C (350°F, Gas Mark 4), for 30 minutes, or until risen and just firm to the touch. Leave to cool in the tin.

4 Cut the sponge into wedges and drizzle extra maple syrup over the top and serve it with spoonfuls of soya yogurt.

3 small ripe bananas

6 tablespoons maple syrup, plus extra to serve

50 g (2 oz) caster sugar

finely grated rind of 1 lemon

125 g (4 oz) soya spread

2 eggs

200 g (7 oz) self-raising flour

2 tablespoons unblanched almonds, chopped

natural soya yogurt, to serve

NUTRITIONAL VALUES
353 kcals
6 g protein (1.3 g soya protein)
19 g fat
3 g saturated fat
1.2 g fibre

Vanilla Panna Cotta with Rhubarb Compote

Preparation time 20 minutes,
plus chilling

Cooking time 5 minutes

Serves 6

For best results use early season rhubarb, while it is still pink and tender. Mature rhubarb loses its delicate colour and will probably need additional sweetening.

750 g (1½ lb) rhubarb, trimmed and cut into 1.5-cm (¾-inch) lengths

275 g (9 oz) caster sugar

2 cinnamon sticks

3 tablespoons water

1 teaspoon powdered gelatine or vegetarian gelling agent

350 g (11½ oz) silken tofu

250 g (8 oz) mascarpone cheese

1 teaspoon vanilla extract

150 ml (¼ pint) double cream

NUTRITIONAL VALUES
461 kcals
12 g protein (5 g soya protein)
24 g fat
14 g saturated fat
2 g fibre
Good source of phytoestrogens

1 Lightly oil 6 small dariole moulds or 150 ml (¼ pint) metal pudding moulds. Put the rhubarb in a heavy-based pan with 175 g (6 oz) of the sugar, the cinnamon sticks and 1 tablespoon of the water. Heat gently, stirring, until the sugar has dissolved. Cover the pan and simmer the mixture gently for 3–4 minutes, until the rhubarb is tender but not falling apart. Transfer the compote to a bowl and leave to cool.

2 Sprinkle the gelatine over the remaining water in a small bowl and leave it to stand. Put the tofu in a food processor with the remaining sugar and blend the mixture until it is smooth, scraping it down from the sides of the bowl.

3 Gently melt the mascarpone in a medium, heavy-based pan until it is runny. Stir the soaked gelatine into the cheese until it is completely dissolved. Pour into a bowl and beat in the vanilla, tofu mixture and cream. Divide the mixture between the moulds and chill them for at least 4 hours until set.

4 Loosen the edges of the moulds with a knife and turn the puddings onto serving plates. Serve with the rhubarb compote.

Index

Page numbers in *italics*
refer to illustrations

ACKNOWLEGEMENTS

Executive Editor: Sarah Ford
Editor: Kate Tuckett
Executive Art Editor: Karen Sawyer
Designer: Jane Forster
Photographer: Lis Parsons
Recipe Writer and Home Economist:
  Joanna Farrow
Nutritionist: Tanya Carr
Stylist: Liz Hippisley
Production Controller: Nigel Reed

Photography:
©Octopus Publishing Group/Lis Parsons

Other Photography:
Alamy/Nigel Cattlin 7 right/Steve Smith
  17 right
Getty Images/Victoria Pearson 13 right

Author Acknowledgements:
A huge thank you to Elphee Medici
whose professional and dietetic
experience have greatly contributed
to the quality of information drawn
together on this enormously topical
and often controversial subject.